Making Dining Furniture

MAKING DINING FURNITURE

Edited by V.J. Taylor

ARGUS BOOKS

Argus Books
Argus House
Boundary Way
Hemel Hempstead
Hertfordshire HP2 7ST
England

First published by Argus Books 1991

ISBN 0 85242 988 6

Phototypesetting by Photoprint, Torquay, Devon
Printed in England by Clays Ltd, St Ives plc

CONTENTS

INTRODUCTION

This is a companion book to *Making Dining Chairs* and follows a similar style of presentation, each design being accompanied by an explanatory text, dimensioned drawings, diagrams that help to clarify difficult points, and a cutting list with measurements in both imperial and metric.

The *Woodworker* magazine has enjoyed a reputation for offering attractive and useful designs to its readers for many years. The thirty-six examples of dining furniture included in this book have been carefully chosen from the large number that have appeared in past issues and we have tried to make the selection as comprehensive as possible.

Thus, we have not only included smaller pieces such as tea trolleys and snack-stands, but also larger designs of sideboards and dressers of various kinds. Tables, too, are well represented and include those with fixed or extending tops, and several examples of the gateleg type.

Another feature is that we have ensured that in as many cases as possible both period and contemporary styles are shown, so that (for example) there are traditional and modern versions of gateleg tables, dining tables, and dressers.

Any reader wishing to make his own dining furniture will be able to choose from a really wide range in the certain knowledge that everything has been done to make his work as straightforward and trouble-free as possible; we believe that woodwork should be fun with a worthwhile product at the end!

Making Dining Furniture

MEDIEVAL AUMBRY

The aumbry was the original food cupboard of medieval times and the precursor of the modern refrigerator; the pierced 'windows' served to keep food fresh for as long as possible.

Today the aumbry would not be used for its original purpose, but it is ideally suited for the storage of books, drinks or china, and it would certainly fit well into the decor of a house where the

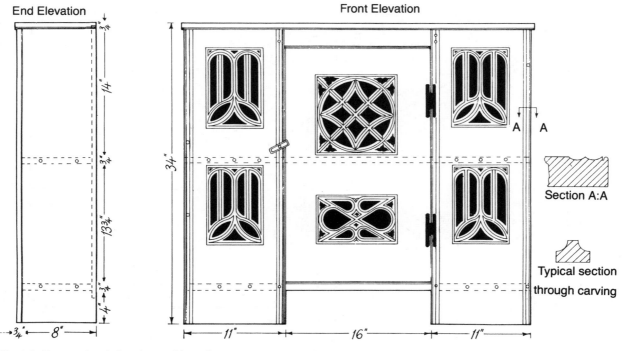

Fig 1.1. Front and end elevations, with sections.

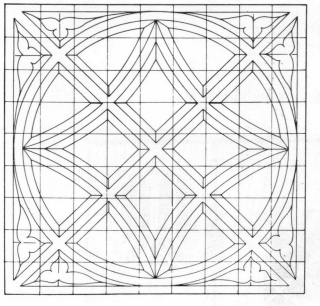

Fig. 1.2. One-inch squared drawing of upper door carving.

Fig. 1.3. One-inch squared drawing of lower door carving.

surroundings are traditional. With its simple natural surfaces and pierced ornamentation it is an attractive piece of furniture and one which employs a variety of processes and skills.

As the piece is made from solid stuff throughout (even the back) there are no framing problems, and you should start with the door. After cutting to size, mark out the Gothic traceries in accordance with the details shown in the drawings, Figs, 1.2, 1.3 and 1.4.

The pierced areas should be removed by drilling and their edges cleaned up with a chisel or a gouge, as required. Next, a small gouge is used to fillet the ribs, and you can see the profile from the section drawing. Note that the back of the door is reduced in thickness locally behind the windows to improve the delicacy of the tracery, and this is best achieved with a flat gouge.

Do not try to be too fussy or precise with the carving. Remember the originals were made centur-

ies ago when tools were cruder than they are today, and much of the appeal of the carving is due to this. The main aims, therefore, should be crisp edges and delicacy of proportion – all tool marks should be left to contribute to the general effect and glasspaper should never be used in any circumstances.

The side fronts should be tackled next and you can proceed with these on the same lines as for the door. The edges of the fronts are fluted as shown, and the extreme edges are lipped with a small moulding, as

Fig. 1.4. One-inch squared drawing of side front carvings.

detailed. If you do not have a moulding plane or electric router to do the job make up a simple scratch tool by grinding a small blade of steel to the required shape. Sandwich this between two wooden blocks which can be held together with bolts and wing-nuts, and scratch the oak sides to the required depth.

Now you can connect the side fronts to the side pieces by dowelling in the conventional manner. You could cheat a little here and use screws well recessed into the fronts – then fill the recesses with oak pegs, leaving them slightly proud of the surface to act as decoration.

The top rail above the door is tenoned into the two side fronts and sides and pegged. The bottom is fitted next after it has been recessed to take the side fronts; it is then screwed and pegged in place.

Shelves are fitted in the positions required to suit whatever storage arrangements you have in mind. Fit the top next, screwing it and pegging it with the pegs cut off flush or as it is solid, use the buttoning method to allow for movement.

The back, which should also be solid timber of a type in keeping with the period, could be made up from elm boards for economy, rub-jointing the pieces to get the width.

Next you can fit and hang the door, using good quality wrought iron hinges as shown, or something similar. The door is secured by a simple wooden turn-button.

A natural finish would be the authentic one. Use linseed oil, well rubbed in and left for a few days to penetrate the oak; then a good quality wax polish applied with a lint-free cloth, bringing it to a polish with a soft, short-haired brush.

CUTTING LIST

	INCHES			MM		
	L	W	T	L	W	T
2 side fronts	34½	11¼	¾	876	286	19
1 door	27½	16¼	¾	698	413	19
1 top	39	9	¾	990	228	19
2 ends	34½	8¼	¾	876	209	19
1 rail at top of Door	18½	2¼	¾	470	58	19
1 bottom piece	38½	8¼	¾	978	209	19
1 shelf	38½	8¼	¾	978	209	19
5 back pieces, each	38½	8¼	½	978	209	12

All parts in oak except the back pieces, which are in elm. Working allowances have been made to lengths and widths; thicknesses are net.

GELDERLAND DROP-LEAF TABLE

This drop-leaf table comes from the Province of Gelderland in Holland, and probably dates back to the 18th century. As was usual with country vernacular furniture, it was made completely from pine, and finished with paint to extend its life. This particular example was in plain red, with the leaves plain green, and a three inch band of red around the edges. In this design, two of the four legs are split down the middle, an ingenious approach to gatelegged construction.

CUTTING LIST

	INCHES			MM		
	L	W	T	L	W	T
4 half legs	31	3¾	1¾	787	96	45
2 legs	31	3¾	3½	787	96	90
1 top bed	42¾	16¾	1	1087	426	25
2 leaves	42¾	20½	1	1087	521	25
2 long rails	36⅝	5⅜	⅞	930	136	22
1 short rail	10⅜	5⅜	⅞	262	136	22
2 long underframe rails	32	3⅜	1¾	812	86	44
2 short underframe rails	10⅜	3⅜	1¾	262	86	44
2 gate lower rails	23¼	1	⅞	590	26	22
2 gate upper rails	23¼	5⅜	⅞	590	136	22
2 gate short rails	9⅛	5⅜	⅞	232	136	22
2 fillets on leaves	18¾	2	½	480	50	12
1 drawer rail	8⅜	1¾	⅞	212	46	22
2 drawer bearers	14¼	5⅛	½	360	130	12
1 drawer front	8⅜	3¾	⅞	212	96	22
2 drawer sides	37½	3¾	½	950	96	12
1 drawer bottom	37½	3¾	¼	950	96	6

Working allowances have been made to lengths and widths; thicknesses are net.

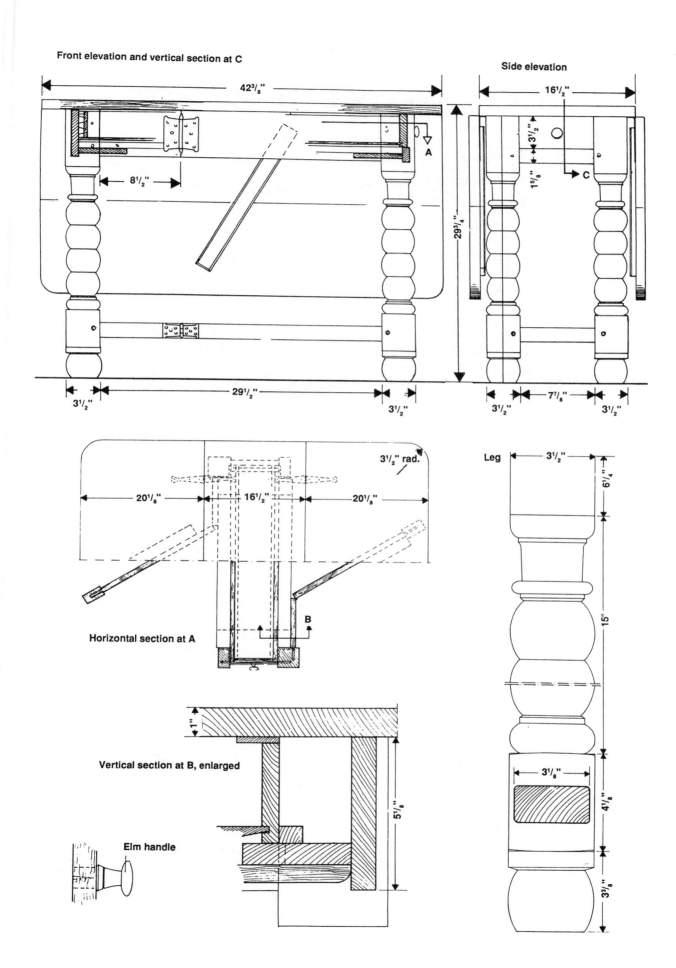

Front elevation and vertical section at C

42³/₈"

29³/₄"

8¹/₂"

A

29¹/₂"

3¹/₂"

3¹/₂"

Side elevation

16¹/₂"

3¹/₂"

1⁵/₈"

C

3¹/₂"

7⁷/₈"

3¹/₂"

3¹/₂"

3¹/₂"

Horizontal section at A

20¹/₈"

16¹/₂"

20¹/₈"

3¹/₂" rad.

B

Vertical section at B, enlarged

1"

5¹/₈"

Elm handle

Leg

3¹/₂"

6¹/₄"

15"

3¹/₈"

4¹/₈"

3³/₈"

5

JACOBEAN-STYLE DRAW TABLE

Fig. 3.1. Tables of this type have been in constant use over the last 400 years, and reproductions are still being made.

The most important feature of this Jacobean table is the bulbous leg. You will probably find it impossible to get six inch squares from which to turn the complete leg as was done in the old days, so you will need to build up by means of blocks to obtain a sufficient thickness of wood.

BUILT-UP LEGS

One method of doing this is shown at (D), Fig. 3.3. The cores of the squares are 3½in thick, and are carried right through the length of the legs; you will have to apply blocks all round where the bulb occurs. These blocks must be of mild timber, carefully selected and well matched; the joints must be good and preferably dowelled. To avoid the likelihood of the joints opening after turning, glue and joint the blocks in place so that the grain has a tendency to curl inwards and so tighten the joints at the surface.

You can, however, use another method, which is to turn the legs in three pieces, the upper and lower sections being pinned to the bulb (see end view, Fig. 3.3). You would be well advised to leave the drilling of the holes in the bulbous section until the leg is in the lathe, as they must be perfectly central and perpendicular. So draw up a full-size detail drawing of the turning with the squares carefully marked, leaving enough timber for the tenons that fit into the bases.

LONGITUDINAL RAILS

With such heavy legs, it is necessary to have a long rail (L) at the top to tie the legs together; the stretcher

(K) admittedly holds the feet together at the bottom but gives little lateral stability. When you have turned up the legs, cut the twin-tenons that joint

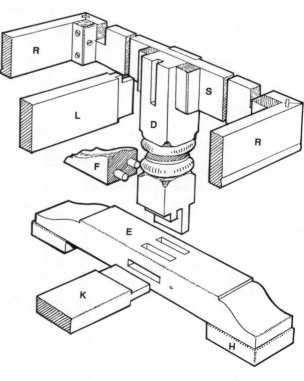

Fig. 3.2. Exploded view of joints and construction of frame, leg, and stretcher.

6

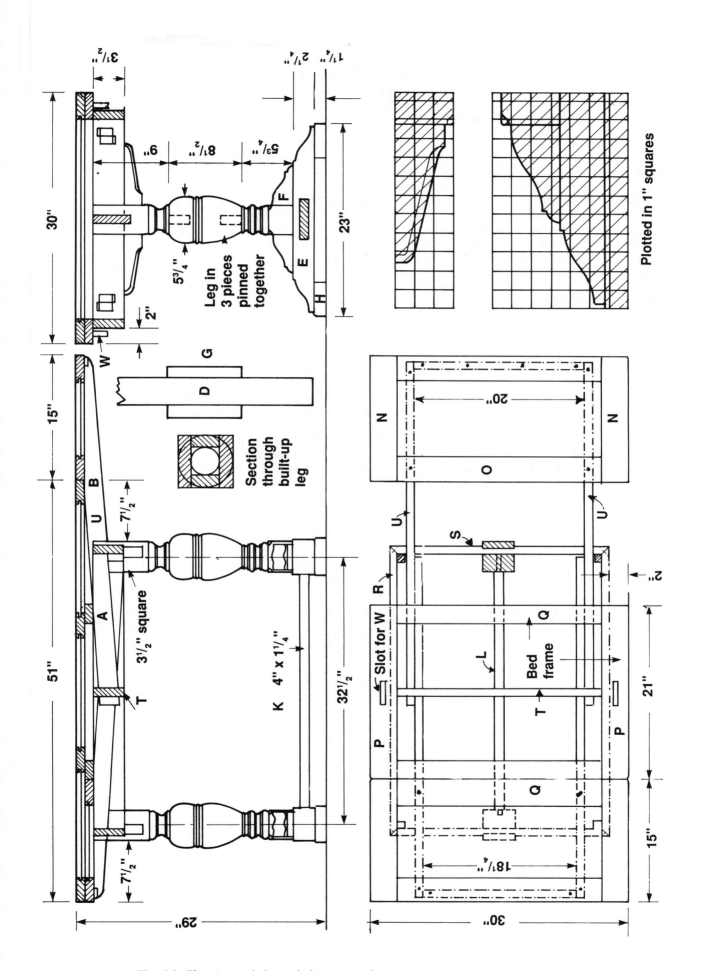

Fig. 3.3. Elevations and plan with dimensions; also one-inch grid drawing of shaped parts.

7

them into the feet, noting that one tenon penetrates right through while the other stops short of the stretcher tenon which passes under it to butt against the other. Cut a bridle joint at the tops of the legs to marry them up with the frieze rails (S), and also mortise them for the long rail (L). The shapes of the feet (E) are shown plotted in one inch squares; you can glue and screw on the shoes (H) underneath.

UNDERFRAMING

This comprises the four frieze rails mitred and tongued at each corner, and the central cross-rail (T) slip-dovetailed or housed to the side frieze rails. You will have to halve this rail (T) over the long rail (L) where the intersection occurs; leave the joint as long as possible for the glue to set and certainly until you cut the holes for, and fit, the slides. Glue and screw a substantial block into each corner of the frieze frame to strengthen the joints.

TOP AND LEAVES

In this type of table, these are usually framed and panelled, the frames being mortised and tenoned together and the panels tongued to the framing. A small bead was sometimes worked along the joints across a table with a solid top to conceal any shrinkage that might occur, and this is worth doing. If, however, you are using plywood for the panels it would be better to omit the bead, as a clean, flush top looks better.

A bed frame (P) and (Q) is located under the top and centrally between the leaves; it is the same thickness as the top and the leaves and you can mortise and tenon the parts together.

You will need to through-mortise the end rails to receive the positioning pieces (W) that are fixed to the main top; then glue and screw the whole frame to the frieze rails (R).

SLIDES

Choose straightgrained beech or a similar timber for these. You will have to cut, shape, and trim these so that they can pass each other through the slots made for them through the cross rail (T). Note that one pair is closer together at one end of the table by the

thickness of the opposite pair. Take care not to cut the slots in the end frieze rails too deeply for the slides; with the main top in position, gradually ease away the slots until the top edge of each slide contacts points (A) and (B), Fig. 3.2. You can then level off

CUTTING LIST

	INCHES			MM		
	L	W	T	L	W	T
D 2 legs	26	3¾	3½	660	95	89
E 2 feet	23½	4⅛	2¼	597	105	58
F 2 brackets	5½	3½	2¼	140	89	58
G 4 leg laminations	9	3¾	1¼	229	95	32
4 leg laminations	9	6¼	1¼	229	159	32
H 4 shoes	4¾	4½	1¼	121	114	32
J 2 brackets	7½	2½	1¼	191	64	32
K 1 stretcher	33½	4¼	1¼	851	108	32
L 1 long rail	33½	4¼	1⅛	851	108	29
M 2 top frame rails	51½	3¼	1⅛	1308	83	29
N 2 top frame rails	15½	3¼	1⅛	393	83	29
O 8 top frame rails	27½	3¼	1⅛	698	83	29
P 2 bed frame rails	21½	3¼	1⅛	546	83	29
Q 2 bed frame rails	27½	2½	1⅛	698	64	29
R 2 frieze rails	34¾	3¾	1	883	95	25
S 2 frieze rails	26½	3¾	1	673	95	25
T 1 cross rail	25¼	3¾	1	642	95	25
U 4 slides	42½	2¾	1	1080	70	25
8 blocks	4	1¼	1	102	32	25
W 2 locating pieces	3½	3	⅝	89	76	16
X 3 top panels, each	25¼	14	½	642	356	13
Y 2 leaf panels, each	25¼	10	½	642	254	13

Working allowances have been made to lengths and widths; thicknesses are net.

the top edges to the horizontal so that you can attach the leaves.

Finally, screw small blocks to act as stops on the undersides of all the slides to prevent them being drawn out too far; also, screw on finger pulls beneath the leaves at each end.

DINING TABLE WITH SHAPED STANDARD ENDS

The table is finished in hard gloss paint, a surface that is very hard-wearing and which has the advantage that the colour may be changed to suit the decor of the room. The timber is Parana pine, relatively cheap, yet giving a solid feel to furniture manufactured from it; it also planes easily, which is a real necessity when dealing with the large surfaces on this job. The drawings are largely self-explanatory, but some notes will undoubtedly be useful.

CHOOSING AND MARKING THE PIECES FOR THE TOP

First of all cut the pieces of 8in board to length as shown in the cutting list, and then label each piece clearly as to its purpose. Clean up the end grain of each piece to make sure that when joined the pieces have 'opposing' warping tendencies – that is, with the annual rings facing in opposite directions.

JOINTING AND GLUING

Prepare the four pieces for the top with a try-plane for edge jointing, and mark each piece appropriately to avoid confusion. The same applies to the three pieces for each section.

Make sure that all the joints pull together evenly, and then glue and cramp them up firmly with, say, three cramps on the top and two for each end.

The next stage is the preparation of the three rails; plane these to exact measurements and square them off to the correct length as shown. Don't forget to allow for tenons in the 1in timber.

After the glue has set thoroughly, uncramp the top and ends and mark out the maximum dimensions required; the top must be a rectangle 57in by 30in, and the ends 29in by 22in. Take care when squaring

up the ends, as a mistake could easily ruin a good piece of work; try to get the rectangles symmetrical about the centre joints/boards of the top/ends respectively.

SHAPING THE TOP

Probably the best way to do this is to make a cardboard template from the 1in squared drawing on the plan view, and then draw round it at each corner. Cut the corner off with a power sabre saw or a bowsaw, and then use a smoothing plane and a spokeshave to shape down to the line, checking frequently that the shape is symmetrical. This is all best done before planing the surface, because after cutting the corners there is less wood to work on.

PLANING AND PAINTING THE TOP AND ENDS

This is a marathon planing exercise! Hold one edge of the top to the bench with G-cramps (using protective blocks, of course) and plane the whole length of the opposite side. When completed, turn the top round and repeat the operation.

Use a smoothing plane to bring both surfaces to a final finish; the results of your efforts here will either make or mar the table as a respectable piece of furniture. Next, round off the edge to suit your taste, using a spokeshave followed by a sequence of glass-papering; if you make a cardboard template of the profile it will ensure the same section all round. When you have finished, paint the work immediately, as the sooner a large area of timber is sealed on all surfaces, exposed or not, the less chance of warping there is.

The ends are shaped and planed next, but not

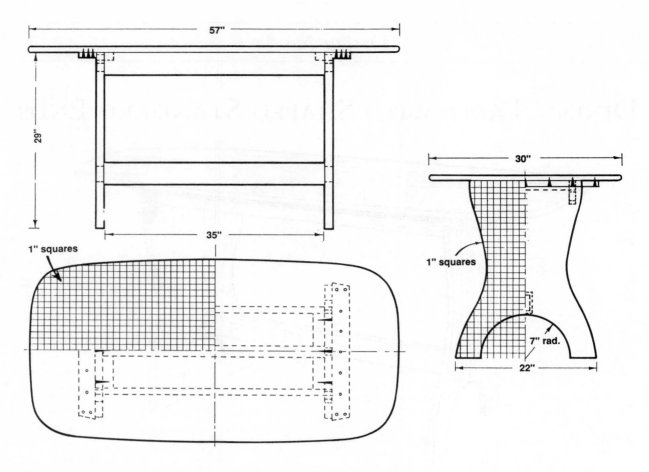

Fig. 4.1. Side and end elevations, with plan. Drawings are squared off to represent one-inch squares

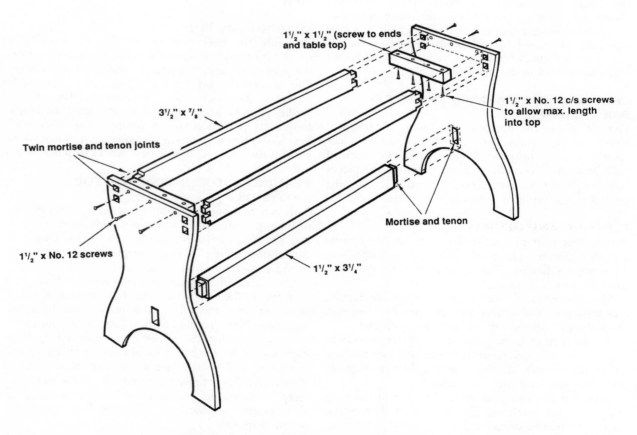

Fig. 4.2. Exploded view of assembly and construction.

painted at this stage. Use exactly the same method for marking them out as for shaping the top, using a cardboard template and drawing the shape for the semicircular cut-out with a pair of compasses.

MAKING THE FRAME

The next step is to mark out the mortise and tenon joints on the frame, 2in by 1in full-width tenons on the top rails, 2¾in by 1in on the bottom rail. Worked in the standard way this is a short process, as is cutting out; take care not to split the timber on the upper mortises as they are fairly near the edge.

When all six joints fit perfectly, make a trial run with cramps to check that all shoulders close up evenly and that the diagonals are equal. Saw a groove in each of the tenons to take a wedge when gluing. Clean up the inside faces of all the parts, and then glue and cramp them up, driving a small wedge home on each tenon. A total of four cramps is recommended – one for each of the upper rails, and one on either side of the lower rail.

At this stage, you can prepare the battens for holding the top firm (3in by ⅞in by 23in), and the ones for holding it down (1½in by 1½in by 12½in). The square section ones should be drilled four times with a ¼in dia drill for fixing to the top; the end sections of the frame are next, drilled three times (¼in dia) for fixing these battens to them. Cut the longer battens to size, shaping off the edges to match the contour of the table top edge and bevel them off to give a neat appearance. Drill ¼in dia countersunk holes, as on the drawing, for fixing to the top. At this juncture, paint the battens and the framework/base after cleaning all surfaces and joints with a plane and/or glasspaper.

FINAL ASSEMBLY

Don't attempt this until all surfaces have had the requisite coats of paint and are thoroughly hard. The battens for holding the top firm should be screwed home first. Use 1¼in screws, making sure that the battens are positioned just either side of the end frames – see the elevation on the drawing. Screw the shorter battens to the inside of the end frames, also with 1½in screws, and then place the top upside down on floor or bench top. Once the frame has been positioned accurately and symmetrically, screw the top down after counterboring holes to a suitable depth for 1½in screws – remember to allow for compression of the wood when tightening up the screws.

CUTTING LIST

	INCHES			MM		
	L	W	T	L	W	T
4 top pieces	58	8	⅞	1473	203	22
6 end pieces	30	8	⅞	761	203	22
1 top rail (cuts two, each 3½in wide)	38	8	⅞	965	203	22
1 top batten (cuts two, each 3in wide)	23	8	⅞	584	203	22
1 lower rail	38	3¼	1½	965	83	38
2 battens for fixing top	12½	1¾	1½	318	45	38

Working allowances have been made to lengths and widths; thicknesses are net.

FINAL NOTES

The table is now complete, but there are a few points to bear in mind, as follows: any paint finish must be applied as soon as possible to prevent warping; all assembly other than glued joints should be done after painting; and all clearance holes for screws should be made slightly oversize to accommodate any small movement of the timber.

TRESTLE TABLE WITH STANDARD ENDS

Fig. 5.1. The extended size is 66in by 30in, closing to 42in by 30in. The table can be easily dismantled and stored away if necessary.

A particular feature of this table is that you can dismantle it when negotiating narrow doorways or passages, or for storage as the stretcher and legs are easily removed from the table framing.

CONSTRUCTION

Prepare the legs (E) to length and width and taper them as shown in Fig. 5.3, the edges being rounded off as shown in the enlarged section. Notch the tops slightly to fit over the frieze rails (H); they are fixed to them by carriage bolts with fly nuts and washers, Fig.5.2. The tenons at the bottom of the legs are carried through the shaped feet (D) and could be pegged. Shape the feet as plotted in the 1in squared drawing, and round off the corners neatly.

THE FRIEZE RAILS

These are marked (G–H) and you could mitre and tongue, or use through dovetails, to join them together at the corners; the dovetails need to be cut carefully for a decorative finish. The cross rail (J) is slip-dovetailed or housed to the side frieze rails centrally.

THE SLIDES

These should be in clean, straight grained timber. They pass one another through the holes cut through the centre cross rail (J). The positions of the holes and the depths of the slots cut into the end frieze rails (H) are controlled by the widths of the slides and their contact with points (A) and (B), Fig. 5.3. One pair of slides is closer together by the thickness of the opposite pair so that they pass one another within the table framework. Each pair of slides is levelled off horizontally to take the leaf to which it is screwed.

STRETCHER (F)

You can find the shoulder length of this from the legs after they have been bolted to the frieze rails. Bevel and round off the top edges with the plane, and shape the bottom edge as shown; alternatively, you can work it with a diminishing bevel to give much the same appearance. The tusks are then taken through the legs, the ends being shaped and rounded. Use rectangular or half-round tapering pegs to hold the legs to the stretcher. You must take care that these joints are made firmly and carefully as the stability of the table depends on them.

TOP AND LEAVES

If you use veneered blockboard, then the edges should ideally be clamped; as an alternative, chipboard would need lippings glued and pinned to the edges, Fig 5.3. Both clamps or lippings should be mitred at the corners and slightly rounded. A bed frame (P) and (Q) is fitted between the leaves, beneath the main top. This is the same thickness as the top and leaves, and is mortised and tenoned

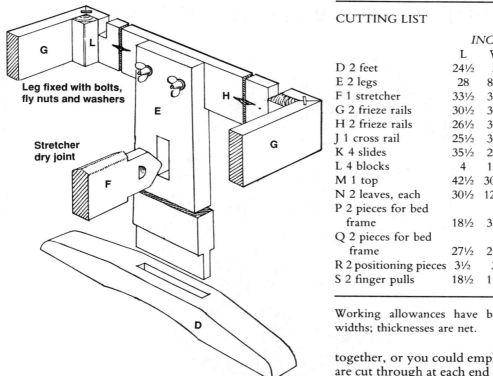

Leg fixed with bolts, fly nuts and washers

Stretcher dry joint

Fig. 5.2. Exploded view of frame, standard end, and stretcher

CUTTING LIST

		INCHES			MM	
	L	W	T	L	W	T
D 2 feet	24½	3	2	622	77	51
E 2 legs	28	8¼	1⅜	711	210	35
F 1 stretcher	33½	3¼	1¼	851	83	32
G 2 frieze rails	30½	3¾	⅞	775	95	22
H 2 frieze rails	26½	3¾	⅞	673	95	22
J 1 cross rail	25½	3¾	⅞	648	95	22
K 4 slides	35½	2½	⅞	903	64	22
L 4 blocks	4	1⅛	⅞	102	29	22
M 1 top	42½	30¼	¾	1079	768	19
N 2 leaves, each	30½	12¼	¾	775	311	19
P 2 pieces for bed frame	18½	3¼	¾	470	83	19
Q 2 pieces for bed frame	27½	2½	¾	698	64	19
R 2 positioning pieces	3½	3	⅝	89	77	16
S 2 finger pulls	18½	1¼	½	470	32	13

Working allowances have been made to lengths and widths; thicknesses are net.

together, or you could employ dowelled joints. Slots are cut through at each end to receive the positioning pieces of the main top, and finally the frame is well screwed to the frieze rails.

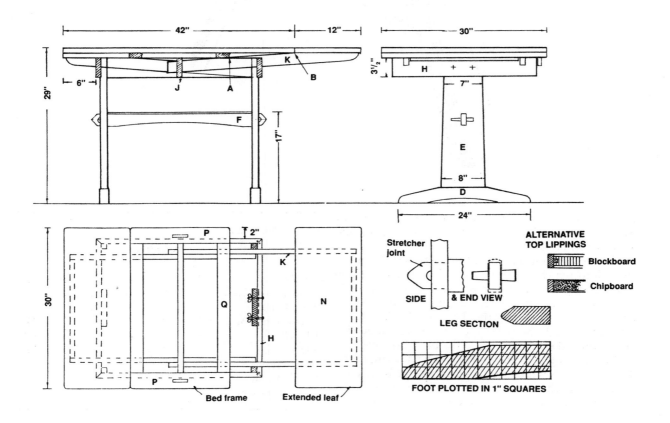

Fig. 5.3. Elevations and plan, with constructional details.

OAK TRIPOD TABLE WITH A TILTING TOP

This is a Dutch country-style table dating back to the Middle Ages, which originated in the Gelderland province in Holland.

The most important part of the design is the heavy block into which the three legs are tongued, and on to which the circular top is pivoted. When the top is in the vertical position it rests against two of the legs; when it is lowered to the horizontal, the peg is inserted through the slit in the strut on the underside of the top and into a slot cut in the block to receive it.

Construction is clearly shown in the drawings, and the only point which needs emphasising is that the direction of the grain in the top pieces must be alternated as shown in the elevation.

CUTTING LIST

	INCHES			*MM*		
	L	W	T	L	W	T
1 top centre board	40⅜	7⅛	⅞	1025	180	22
6 top boards from	197	6⅛	⅞	5000	156	22
2 top bearers	39⅜	2¼	1¼	1000	56	32
1 cross rail (slotted)	11¼	2¼	1	285	56	25
1 block	11¼	10½	4	285	266	102
3 legs	26⅛	3⅜	1⅜	662	86	35
1 underframe rail	20½	2⅝	1¼	520	66	32
1 underframe rail	17¾	2⅝	1¼	450	66	32
1 peg from scrap						

Working allowances have been made to lengths and widths; thicknesses are net.

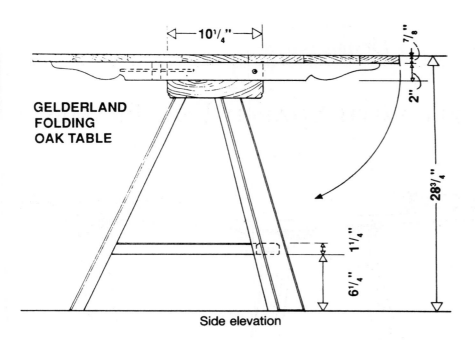

**GELDERLAND
FOLDING
OAK TABLE**

10¼"

⅞"

2"

28¾"

1¼"

6¼"

Side elevation

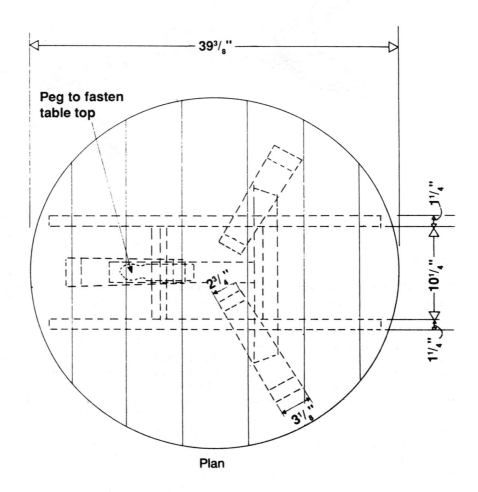

39⅜"

Peg to fasten
table top

1¼"

10¼"

1¼"

2¾"

3⅛"

Plan

DINING TABLE WITH SHAPED END FRAMES

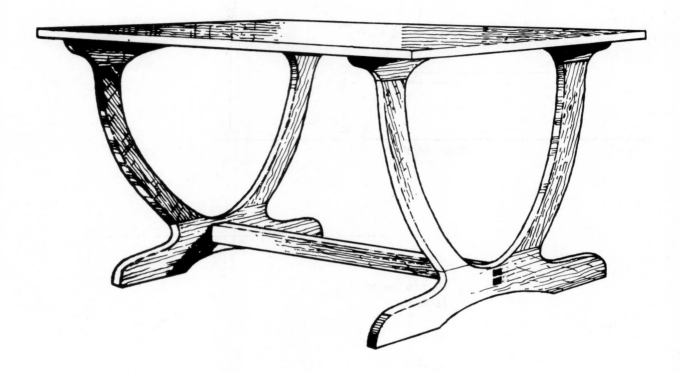

This is a table built in the solid, honest style that is just right for the English oak in which it was made. It takes six chairs comfortably, with room for more if you wish.

MARKING OUT AND MAKING THE FRAMES
Begin by making the end frames. Plane the two rails and the two legs carefully to width and thickness, checking the squareness of the faces and edges. Saw and plane the top slopes off the foot rail. Lay out the four pieces in the arrangement shown in the squared diagram (Fig. 7.3.), and scribe the shoulder lines from one piece to the other. Also mark the widths of the legs on to the rails. Repeat the procedure with the second end pieces.

Mark out the approximate profile of all shaping on the legs and rails, and then mark out all the mortises and tenons, gauging from the face sides. The tenons are all 2¼in square and ⅜in thick, arranged in pairs (twin tenons) to ensure a large gluing area. Cut the mortises and then the tenons – note that the tenons are all at right angles to their shoulders.

Having tested the fit of these joints dry, return to the shaping of the legs. If you have one, use a bandsaw (or failing this, a bowsaw) to cut the rough profile, leaving a ½in to ¾in solid piece behind the shoulder of each tenon. Do not shape under the feet yet.

Now glue the end frames, using the cramps approximately along the line of the legs. A spacer strip placed between the cramp heads on the top rail will prevent their slipping inwards. Allow the glue to set.

Shape the profile with firmer gouges and spoke-shaves, then round off to the shapes shown in the removed sections in the squared-off drawing – be extra careful to leave flats where the long rails have to be jointed on.

Plane the long rails to a rectangular section 1⅞in by 1⅜in or 2¾in by 1¾in. Mark off the shoulder lines 40¾in apart, allowing 1⅝in at each end of the tenons. The top rail twin tenons are also 1⅜in thick, and cover the full 1⅜in width. The lower rail twin tenons are ½in thick, and again full width. Mark out the mortises on the end frames and cut them, chiselling in halfway from each side for safety; then work the tenons and trim them to fit. You can wedge the joints if you wish.

Test-fit these joints by cramping them up dry; then take them apart, shape the rails, and cut the slots for the buttons. Glue up, checking to see that the table is not in twist; it must stand level.

When the glue is dry, finish off any shaping which has to be done. You'll find a sanding attachment to a power drill is extremely useful for this, especially where the end frame legs and rails meet.

THE TOP
My procedure for this was to edge-joint four or five boards with carefully matched grain patterns. All the

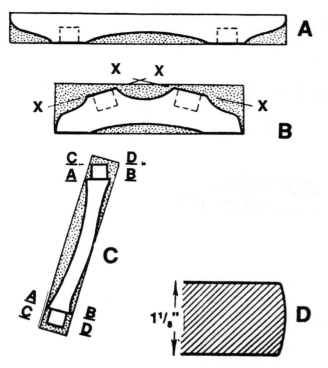

Fig. 7.1. Top end rail is shown at (A); details of foot and lines X–X on shoulders at (B); angles of tenons (C); and section of top (D).

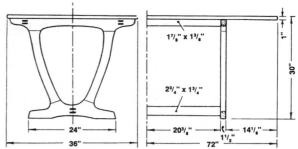

Fig. 7.2. End elevation, and half front elevation.

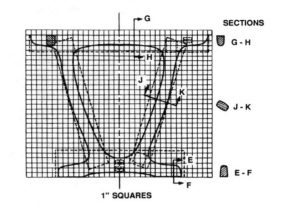

Fig. 7.3. End elevation drawn on one inch grid.

meeting edges have to be planed square and true, as is usual with rub-jointing. I then reinforced the joints with ⅜in dowelling at 6in centres, using a precision tool jig unit that gives great speed and accuracy.

Put as many sash cramps as you have available on the work, alternately above and underneath; one every 9in is a good average.

Plane the underside flat and to a good finish. Planing flat is speedier if you work diagonally at first to iron out the high spots, then follow by working along the grain. Finally, make sure the plane iron is sharp, set it fine and plane out any tears. This is quicker and better than trying to hand-sand to a finish, although this may still be necessary at the very end.

Make the buttons and fix the frame to the top. Put in steel screws first to make pilot holes – later they can be replaced by brass ones. With the whole table now assembled, very carefully plane the top and the edges.

I applied several coats of boiled linseed oil to the table at weekly intervals, using heavy pressure. Several months later I rubbed on a plain wax polish, which was the first of many; English oak responds extremely well to this waxing technique over a period of time.

CUTTING LIST

	INCHES			MM		
	L	W	T	L	W	T
4 legs, end frame	27½	4¼	1½	698	109	38
2 bottom rails, end frame	24½	6¼	1½	622	159	38
2 top rails, end frame	30½	3¾	1½	775	95	38
1 top	72½	36¼	1⅛	1841	921	29
2 long top rails	45½	2¼	1½	1155	58	38
1 underframe rail	45½	3¼	2	1155	83	51

Working allowances have been made to lengths and widths; thicknesses are net.

Hepplewhite-Style Serving Cabinet

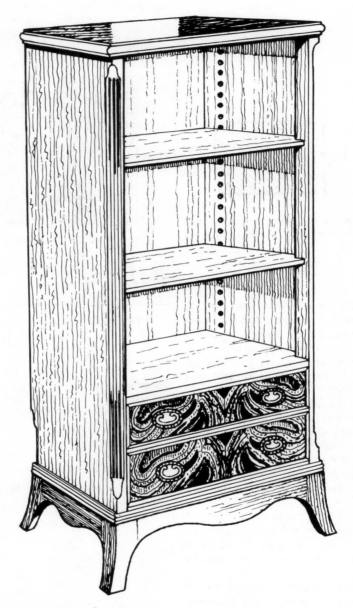

A handsome and useful addition to your dining furniture

This cabinet serves as a sideboard but occupies much less floor space, and is therefore suitable for the smaller dining rooms of today. The shelves carry crockery and table linen while the drawers contain cutlery trays.

THE CARCASE

Plane the pilasters (1) to the section shown in Fig. 2 and plough a groove along one square edge of each. Work four ³/₁₆in wide flutes down the bevelled face of each pilaster, either with a power router or a

scratch stock; the ends are stopped with a gouge cut as in Fig. 3.

Mark out the pilaster block shaping (2), Fig. 4. Use a supporting saddle when bandsawing the curves, and clean off any saw marks. Cut the blocks to length and also diagonally to a triangular section; then glue them in place on the pilasters and level them off when the glue has set.

Next, rebate a tongue on the front edge of the carcase ends (3) to fit the grooves of the pilaster, noting that the pilasters themselves should stand

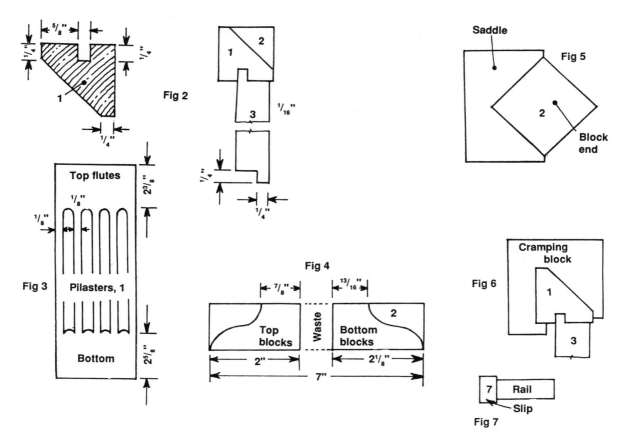

Fig 2

Fig 3

Top flutes

Pilasters, 1

Bottom

Fig 4

Top blocks

Waste

Bottom blocks

Fig 5

Saddle

Block end

Fig 6

Cramping block

Fig 7

Rail

Slip

$\frac{1}{16}$in proud of the faces of the ends. Also, rebate the back edge of the carcase ends for the carcase back to fit into, and glue the pilasters to the ends, using shaped cramping blocks as in Fig. 6. Bear in mind that it is essential for good drawer fitting that the inside faces of the pilasters are parallel with the ends.

Now edge one of the pine top rails (4) with the slip (8); also the bottom rail (5), the drawer rail (6), and the three shelves with the slips (7); plane the waste level when the glue has set. Fig. 8 gives details of the rail end joints. The front rails measure 21½in shoulder to shoulder, and the back rails are 22⅜in. The fixed shelf (9) is tenoned in, as is the drawer rail (6), and is housed ¼in deep across the inside of the ends. Fig. 9 gives the joint positions into the pilasters.

Bore ⅜in dia holes, 1 in apart and ⅜in deep, for the shelf peg supports. You can then glue and cramp up the carcase, checking that it is square diagonally between the top rails and across the front.

THE BASE

First, bandsaw out the feet shapes, noting that the end view of the back feet differs from the other shapes, Fig. 10.

Cut the mortise and tenon joints between the legs and the base rails (11) and (12), and make a test-fit,

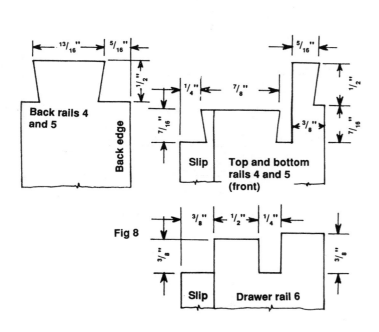

Fig 8

Back rails 4 and 5

Back edge

Slip

Top and bottom rails 4 and 5 (front)

Slip

Drawer rail 6

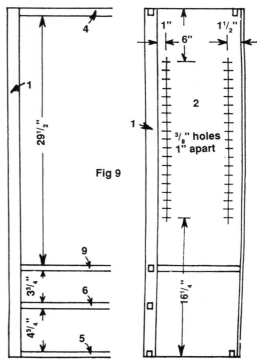

Fig 9

dry, to check that the base frame accurately fits to the carcase bottom end. Mark out and bandsaw the base rails. Clean off and glue up the base frame and flush off the joints.

Use Scotch glue to lay the veneers and start by toothing and sizing the front and end surfaces. Cross-veneer with Cuban curl mahogany or whatever figured veneer you have, working out from the central joints to give a nicely balanced appearance. You can use a thin plywood caul covered with a material such as linoleum, thick felt, or sheet cork to apply even pressure in the leg curves. When the glue has set, the veneers will need cleaning up.

JOINING BASE AND CARCASE

Rebate the top edge of the base frame as in Fig. 13; mitre, and then glue and pin the base moulding (13) into the rebate. Screw the lining pieces (14) inside the base frame and screw through them into the carcase to fasten the two together.

THE DRAWERS

Fit the drawer fronts into the carcase, and tooth and size the face sides as you did for the base front. Cross-veneer in a matching veneer, again working from the central joints, and taking care that these are in line when the fronts are in the carcase. You will find it looks best if the veneers are adjacent pieces from the leaf.

Once the glue has set and you have cleaned up the veneers, you can rebate the drawer fronts for the drawer bottoms as in Fig. 16.

Fig. 17 shows the dovetail spacing for the 3¾in drawer front; you can space out the dovetails for the other drawer front and both drawer backs proportionately. Now rebate the drawer sides for the bottoms, glue up the drawers and temporarily fit and pin the bottoms in place. Flush off the dovetail joints and run in the drawers to test them for fit.

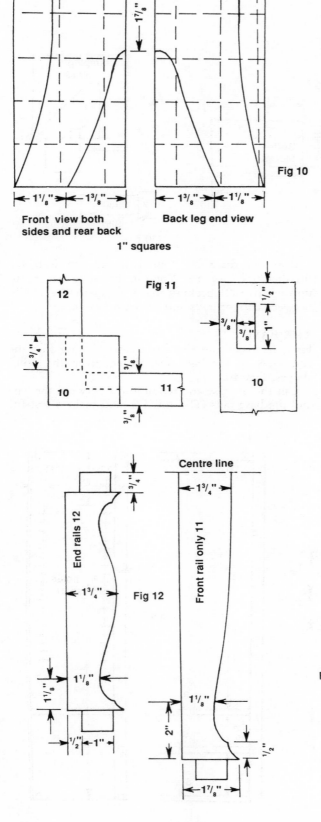

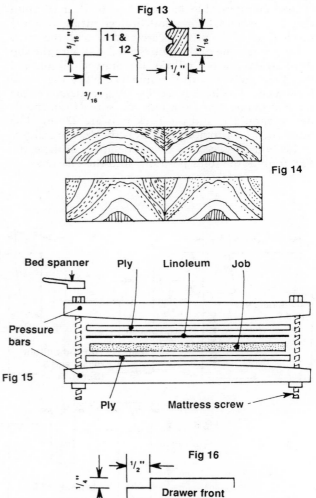

20

Fitting and fixing the drawer runners (2l) and drawer guides (22) comes next, followed by glue-blocking the bottoms into the drawers, taking care that the finished drawers still fit and are square with the carcase

Follow on by rebating the fronts for the cockbeads, the corners of which should be mitred; you can then glue and pin them in place. Also glue and pin the drawer stops (27) on to the front rails so that the drawer fronts are flush with the front rails when the drawers are closed.

THE TRAYS

Fit the tray fronts and backs inside the drawers; the two 2in trays fit into the bottom drawer, and the 3in tray into the top drawer. You will then need to rebate the tray fronts, backs, and ends for the bottoms.

Fig. 21 shows the dovetail spacing for the 3in tray; space out the 2in trays in proportion. Also cut the central hand holes through the tray ends. Plane the tray divisions (30) and (31) to the section shown in Fig. 23; and house the ends of the divisions ⅛in deep

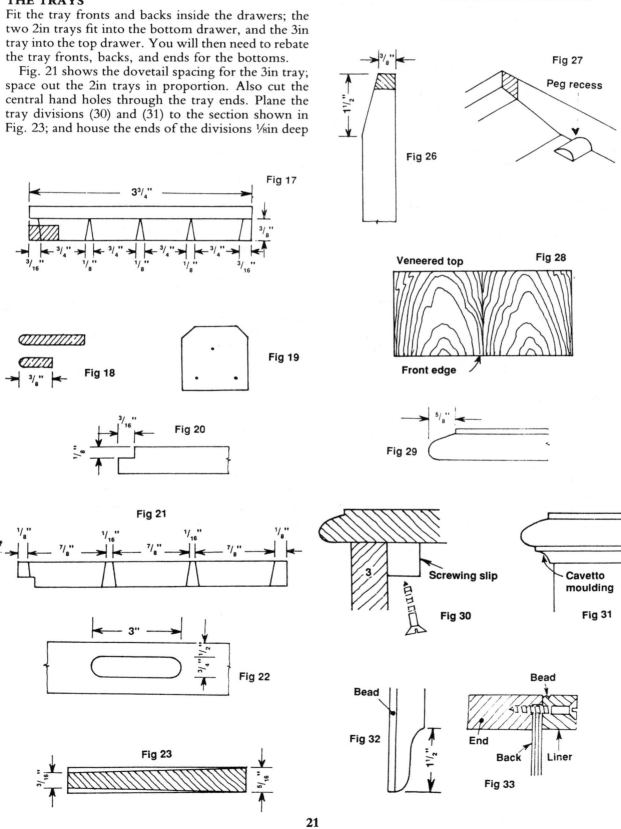

21

into the tray front and backs to give five equal cutlery divisions as in Fig. 25. Glue up the trays, fit in the bottoms and line them with baize, and also glue the rebates. You can now pin up through the bottoms into the fronts, the backs, and the ends; also screw up through the bottoms into the divisions.

THE LOOSE SHELVES

Fit these in and chamfer the front edges. You will need to turn up ten 1in long by ⅜in diameter mahogany pegs which act as shelf supports; also bore semicircular peg recesses on the undersides of the shelves to correspond with the carcase and peg holes.

Glue the top slips (37–39) around the carcase top, and flush them off. Tooth the top side of the assembly and size it thoroughly. Veneer the top side a matching veneer, again jointing the veneers centrally.

Now work a thumb moulding on the ends and the front edges of the top. Fix screwing fillets between the top rails of the carcase, and screw up through them to secure the top to the carcase. The cavetto moulding under the top and around the carcase will need to be mitred at the corners and you can then glue and pin it in place.

Finally, fit and screw in the plywood carcase back. Shape the bottom end of the back liners, and work a ⅛in bead on the outside edge next to the carcase. Fix these liners in place by screwing them and the carcase back into the carcase ends.

CUTTING LIST

		INCHES			MM		
		L	W	T	L	W	T
1	2 pilasters	40¾	1½	1¼	1035	38	32
2	2 pieces for pilaster blocks	7½	1⁵⁄₁₆	1¹⁄₁₆	191	33	27
3	2 carcase ends	40¾	10¼	¾	1035	261	19
4	2 top rails	23⅞	1½	¾	607	38	19
5	2 bottom rails	23⅞	1½	½	607	38	13
6	1 drawer rail	22⅞	1½	½	581	38	13
7	5 front rail and shelf slips	22	1⅛	⅜	559	29	10
8	1 top rail slip	22	1⅜	⅜	559	35	10
9	1 fixed shelf	23½	11⅛	½	597	283	13
10	4 feet	5½	2¾	2½	140	70	64

CUTTING LIST (continued)

		INCHES			MM		
		L	W	T	L	W	T
11	2 front & back base rails	23	2⅛	¾	584	54	19
12	2 end base rails	9½	2⅛	¾	242	54	19
13	1 base moulding	50½	⁹⁄₁₆	¼	1283	14	6
14	1 lining piece	48½	1	¾	1232	25	19
15	1 drawer front	22⅛	4	⅝	562	102	16
16	1 drawer front	22⅛	5	⅝	562	127	16
17	1 drawer back	22⅛	3⅜	⁵⁄₁₆	562	86	8
18	1 drawer back	22⅛	4⅜	⁵⁄₁₆	562	111	8
19	2 drawer sides	11	4	⁵⁄₁₆	279	102	8
20	2 drawer sides	11	5	⁵⁄₁₆	279	127	8
21	4 drawer runners	8	1½	½	203	38	13
22	4 drawer guides	8	1⅛	½	203	29	13
23	2 drawer bottoms, ply	22	10⅜	³⁄₁₆	559	264	5
24	2 cockbeads	22½	1	⅛	571	25	3
25	2 cockbeads	22½	⅝	⅛	571	16	3
26	4 cockbeads	5½	⅝	⅛	140	16	3
27	4 drawer stops	1½	1¼	¼	38	32	6
28	4 tray backs & fronts, each	21½	2¼	⁵⁄₁₆	546	58	8
29	4 tray ends	9¾	2¼	⁵⁄₁₆	248	58	8
30	8 tray divisions	9⅜	2⅛	⁵⁄₁₆	238	54	8
31	2 tray backs & fronts	21½	3¼	⁵⁄₁₆	546	83	8
32	2 tray ends	9¾	3¼	⁵⁄₁₆	248	83	8
33	4 tray divisions	9⅜	2⅞	⁵⁄₁₆	238	73	8
34	3 tray bottoms, ply	21¼	9¼	³⁄₁₆	540	235	5
35	2 loose shelves	23	10¼	¾	584	260	19
36	1 carcase top, ply	24	11¼	¾	609	286	19
37	1 top back slip	24	¾	⅞	609	19	22
38	1 front	26	1¼	⅞	660	32	22
39	2 top end slips	13	1¼	⅞	330	32	22
40	2 screwing slips	8	1	¾	203	25	19
41	1 under-top cavetto moulding	25½	⅝	⅜	648	16	10
42	2 under-top cavetto mouldings	12¾	⅝	⅜	324	16	10
43	1 carcase back, ply	40¾	12¾	¼	1035	324	6
44	2 back liners	37½	1	¾	952	25	19

Working allowances have been made to lengths and widths; thicknesses are net.

WALL CUPBOARD

When my daughter moved house recently she asked me if I could make a wall cupboard to provide extra kitchen storage space. There was already a fitted pine cupboard, but not wanting to work in a softwood I chose olive ash as a harmonising timber. It comes from the heartwood of mature European ash trees, and being marked with dark brown streaks is beautiful in appearance. It glues well, works easily, and is simple to stain and finish, though the interesting grain and colour can make staining unnecessary.

The open shelf adds an attractive feature to an almost square (36in wide by 35⅝in high) front elevation; it is of course possible to adapt the measurements, though watch out for bowing if the cupboard is made much larger.

CONSTRUCTION

As a first step select and plane the material for the two sides, the top and the two cupboard shelves to

a thickness of ⅞in. But plane the open shelf to 1in thick to give extra weight to the lowest moulding and to allow depth for the plate groove.

Using the best grained pieces for the sides, cut and plane the top and sides to 7in wide. Mark out the decorative shapes at the bottom of the side pieces from the grid squares in Fig. 9.1, and cut them out with a bandsaw or a coping saw. File and glasspaper them smooth.

Finish the two shelves to 6in wide, allowing the back (which is ⅜in thick) to be rebated into the inner face of the sides and top. Cut the bottom shelf, which is also rebated to take the back, to the same width as the sides below the decorative feature. To display plates safely on this shelf, work a stopped groove along it with a power router. Experiment to find the optimum position for your plates to stand in the groove.

Cut a recess at the middle of the centre shelf to

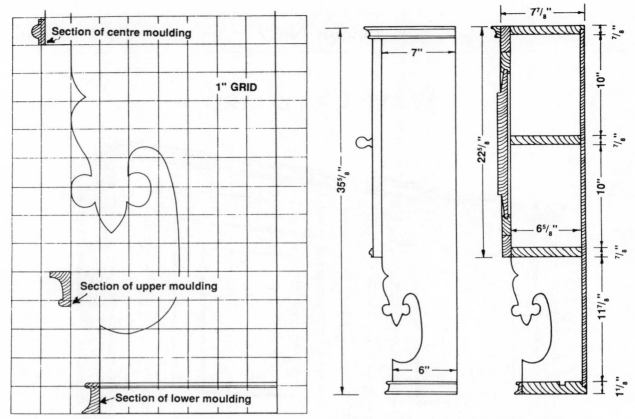

Fig. 9.1. One-inch grid drawing of shaped parts and moulding profiles.

Fig. 9.2. End elevation and sectional rod, with dimensions.

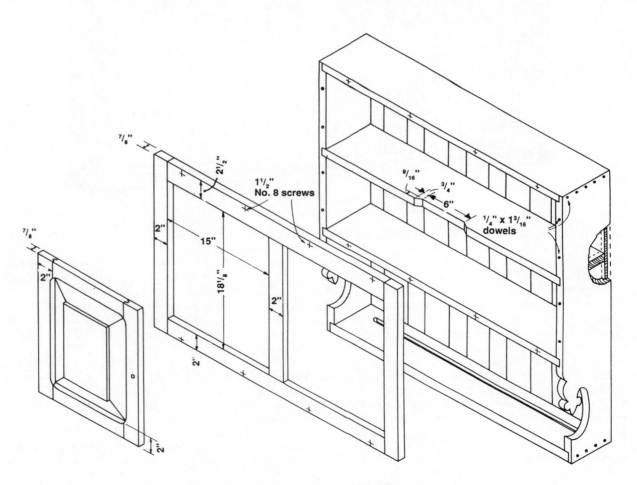

Fig. 9.3. How cupboard is assembled.

provide clearance for the catches that are attached to the backs of the doors and lock on to the upright.

The top and bottom, shelves and sides are joined by means of simple housing joints, worked preferably with a power router. This type of joint is adequate because, after gluing and cramping, you can reinforce the joints at the top and bottom with dowels, the ends of which will be hidden by the applied mouldings.

The back of the cabinet consists of ⅜in ash strips of random widths; these have their edges rebated to overlap each other. You can bevel the edges to create a feature, and to minimise any unsightly gap if shrinkage occurs. Glue and pin the planking into the rebates and to the back of the shelves.

tion, and once the glue has set clean up the cabinet before applying the mouldings.

MOULDINGS
The shape of these depends on your taste and what tools are available to make them with. I made three different mouldings (Fig. 9.2), using a power router fitted with a coving cutter plus a small rebate plane for the upper and lower ones, and a corner-rounding cutter in the router for the central moulding.

Try to use a strong glue on its own to fix the mouldings as pins or nails inevitably leave marks. Remember to make enough of the upper and lower mouldings to go round the corners, which are mitred; trim the centre moulding flush with the sides.

DOOR PANELS AND ASSEMBLY
Cut out the frame rails for these and rout a ⅜in square groove along the inner edges of each for its panel. Unless you are lucky enough to have timber sufficiently wide for the panel, you will of course have to glue up pieces to make the width. Make sure that the edges of the pieces are square and straight,

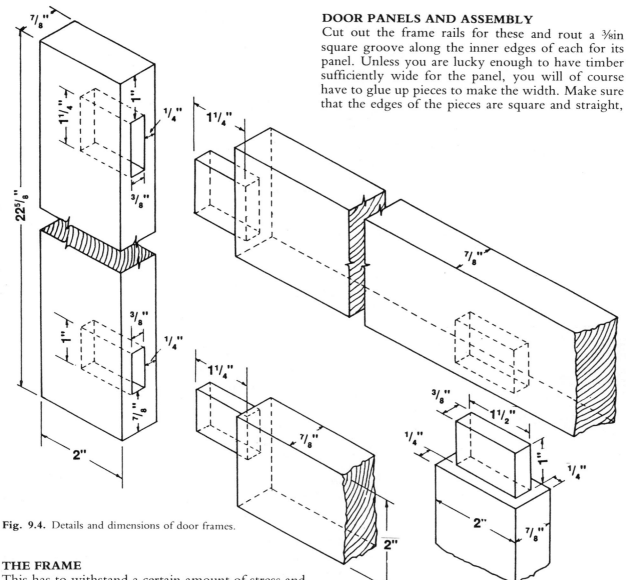

Fig. 9.4. Details and dimensions of door frames.

THE FRAME
This has to withstand a certain amount of stress and is therefore constructed with mortise and tenon joints (Fig. 9.4) which should be cut accurately to impart the greatest strength possible.

Along the top and bottom of the frame, drill and countersink holes for 1½in x 8 screws which you can hide with the mouldings. To supplement the screws, the frame is attached to the sides with dowels. Drill ¼in dia holes, ¾in deep, in the leading face of the sides, and drill corresponding holes in the frame, taking care not to break through the outside.

Now glue, screw, and cramp the frame in posi-

and that when you glue them side by side there is no bowing or sliding in the cramps.

Fielding the panels is tricky. You can do it with a circular saw on which you can angle the fence or blade, or use a power router followed by trimming up with a plane.

Once you have cut the joints of the frame (Fig. 9.5) and bevelled the inner edges for effect, glue up the doors. But do not let any glue get on to the panels

25

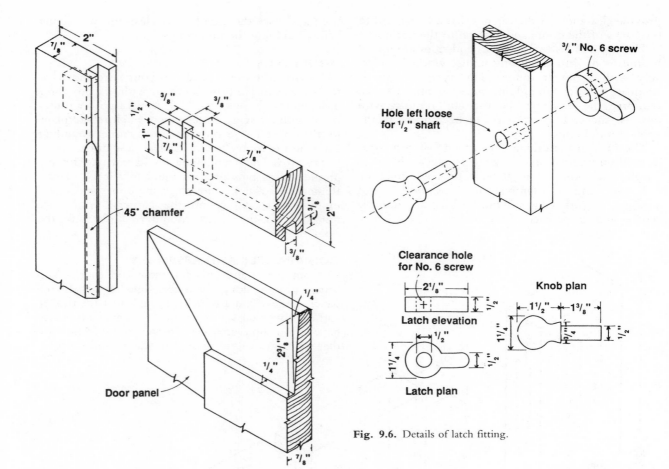

Fig. 9.5. Details and dimensions of door construction.

Fig. 9.6. Details of latch fitting.

as shrinkage is likely to occur, and they must be able to move.

For the same reason of shrinkage, it's best to apply the chosen finish to the panels before you assemble the doors to avoid the chance of any unfinished wood showing later.

FITTING UP

Drill a ½in hole in each door for a knob and catch, and hang it on brass flush hinges. Turn two knobs, drill a ½in hole into each and glue in a ½in dowel (Fig. 9.6); push the dowel through to be a sliding fit, and attach a shaped catch at the other end with a small brass screw.

You can hang the cupboard by means of brass glass plates or one of the several KD fittings available.

CUTTING LIST

	INCHES			*MM*		
	L	W	T	L	W	T
2 ends	34⅛	7¼	⅞	866	184	22
1 top	36¼	6⅞	⅞	921	175	22
2 middle shelves	36¼	6⅞	⅞	921	175	22
1 bottom shelf	36¼	6¼	1	921	159	25
1 back	36	36	⅜	914	914	10
2 corner stiles	23⅛	2¼	⅞	587	58	22
1 central muntin	21⅛	2¼	⅞	536	58	22
1 frieze rail	35½	2¾	⅞	902	70	22
1 lower rail	35½	2¼	⅞	902	58	22
4 door stiles	18⅝	2¼	⅞	473	58	22
4 door rails	18	2¼	⅞	457	58	22
2 panels	15⅜	12¼	⅞	391	311	22
1 top moulding	54	1½	¾	1371	38	19
1 centre moulding	54	1⅛	⅜	1371	29	10
1 bottom moulding	54	1½	⅝	1371	38	16

Working allowances have been made to lengths and widths; thicknesses are net.

DOUBLE CAKE STAND

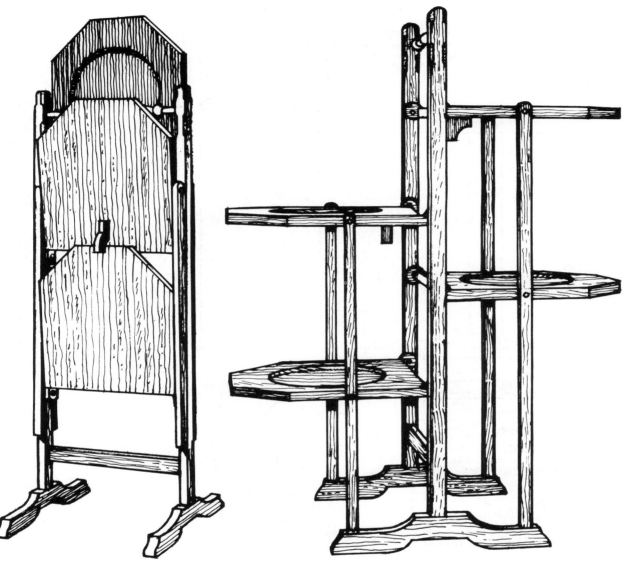

Fig. 10.1. The stand, when closed. Note the button attached to the top tray for catching it over the lower one.

Fig. 10.2. The stand opened for use. No locking system is needed as the weight of the trays is taken by the feet.

In Fig. 10.2 the stand is shown open ready for use. It has four trays with screws acting as pivot connections to the two pillars of the central framing, and four legs screw-pivoted to the edges of the trays retain them in a horizontal position. In Fig. 10.1 it is shown closed, being kept in that position by two turn-buttons screwed to the underside of the two uppermost trays. Working drawings are shown in Figs. 10.3 and 10.4.

FRAMEWORK

The framed section consists of two pillars, the lower ends of which are tenoned to fit into mortises in the two shaped feet. They are glued and wedged together. The two upper ends are bored ½in diameter and ½in deep to receive the ends of the handle. This can be turned or rounded by hand, its two dowel-like ends being glued into the main uprights.

The handle was turned from a piece of padauk, making a pleasing contrast in colour, the rest of the material being figured oak. The straining rail is connected by through mortise and tenon joints, and the tenons project about ³⁄₁₆in and have their ends chamfered all round. An enlarged detail is shown of the framework joints in Fig. 10.4.

TRAYS

These are 11in long, 10in wide, and ¾in thick; and you can dish out their upper faces on a lathe to finish 7in diameter and ³⁄₈in deep.

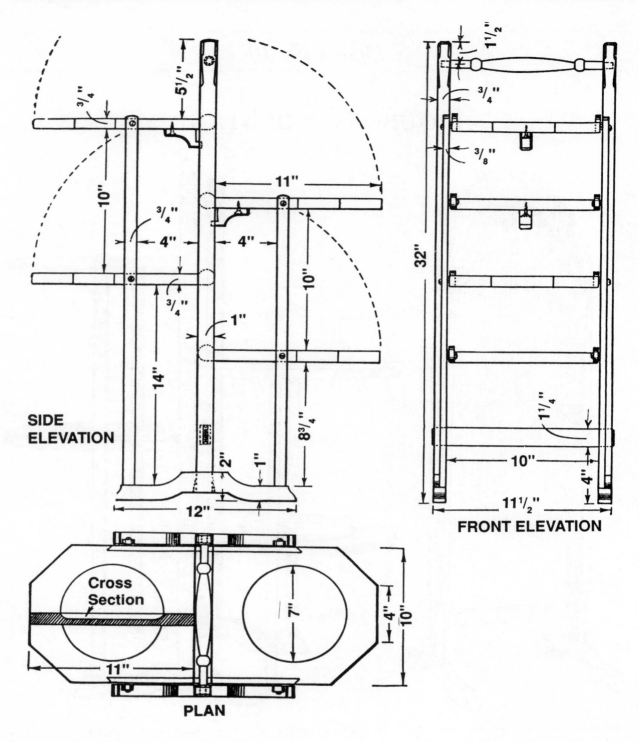

Fig. 10.3. Elevations and plan with principal sizes.

You can do the job by hand in the following manner. Start by describing the circle with the sharpened ends of compass dividers, one end being filed to a cutting edge, the other to a point. You can remove almost all the surplus wood with gouges of various sizes and then work the flat bottom smooth with a router plane and scraper. Cut the hollow along the edge with a small firmer gouge.

A section through a tray is shown in Fig. 10.3 from which you can make a template for the tray bottom, thus ensuring uniformity. Shape the front ends and round the edges as shown in Fig. 10.3

To connect the trays to the pillars, prepare two pivot strips as shown in Figs. 10.3 and 10.4; then cut

matching pieces away from the sides of the trays and fit the strips tightly and glue them. Next shape the wider circular end of each strip and bore a hole centrally to receive the 1in round head brass screws that pivot them to the pillars. Note that the other ends of the strips are cut at angles of about 45 degrees, thus providing a stronger joint. You will need two long and two short legs to complete the job; all four are ¾in wide and ⅜in thick. The longer pair are 25¾in long and the shorter pair 20½in; their upper ends are slightly rounded.

Once you have prepared all the parts, clean them up with a finely set smoothing plane and glasspaper them to a smooth finish.

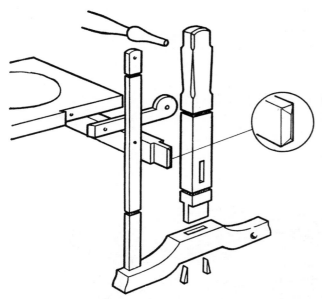

Fig. 10.4. Exploded view of construction.

ASSEMBLY

Glue the stretcher rail and the handle to the pillars and leave the sub-assembly in cramps till the glue has set. Glue the pillar tenons into the mortises of the feet, cramp, and drive in some glued wedges. Attach the four trays to the framework, and the legs to the edges of the trays, with 1in round headed brass screws. Beware of snapping the brass screws when screwing in – it's advisable to insert a steel screw first, withdraw it, and replace it with brass.

Two wood turn buttons keep the stand closed as shown in Fig. 10.3; fix them with screws to the underside of the two upper trays, see Figs. 10.1 and 10.2. The stand illustrated is natural colour, with the grain filled, and finished with wax.

CUTTING LIST

	INCHES			*MM*		
	L	W	T	L	W	T
2 pillars	32½	1¼	¾	825	32	19
1 rail	12½	1½	¾	318	38	19
1 handle	12½	1¼	1	318	32	25
2 feet	12½	2¼	¾	318	58	19
2 supports	26½	1	⅜	673	25	10
2 supports	21	1	⅜	292	261	19
4 trays	11½	10¼	¾	292	261	19
8 tray slips	7½	1½	⅜	190	38	10
2 buttons	3	1½	¾	76	38	19

Working allowances have been made to lengths and widths; thicknesses are net.

CUPBOARD DRESSER

The combination, or universal, woodworker could justly be called the machine of the 80s. For the craftsman woodworker, the advantage of machinery is to supplement hand work; and for the amateur, it means that he can readily attain professional stan-

dards. I hope this cupboard dresser, with its traditional construction, will prove both points.

The machine I used was a Startrite-Robland K260, which consisted of a 10in by 7in planer-thicknesser, a 9in circular saw, a spindle moulder, and a slot mortiser. The planer was fitted with a pair of high-speed steel knives, which was set ready for use. The standard TC 24-tooth sawblade was best suited to ripping and required care when used for crosscutting to avoid spalling (also called 'break out' or 'spelching'), especially when cutting tenon shoulders.

PREPARATION OF TIMBER

After first crosscutting the boards with a hand, a jig, or a crosscut saw, the machine was cleared of all fences to allow a clear area for freehand ripping, the sapwood being removed and the boards split at the same time. Each piece was labelled as it was dealt with, and ticked off on the cutting list; the idea was to finish with all the items on the cutting list crossed off, and a pile of component parts in some sort of order!

It sounds obvious, but when preparing material

you do need to remember the capacity of the plane – in this case 10in. If you need, say, an 18in top or panels 12in wide, they cannot be got out whole even if the timber itself is wide enough.

PLANING AND THICKNESSING

I passed each piece over the surfacer, flattening one side and straightening the edges before putting it through the thicknesser. I found that it's a good idea to lower the thicknessing table to its maximum to allow the chips to escape; a few strokes of a candle over the table made for a smoother feed, and an assistant was useful, too, and saved a lot of footwork.

TENONING

One of the luxuries of machine woodworking is the ability to produce tenons accurately and efficiently and whether you choose to do your tenoning on the

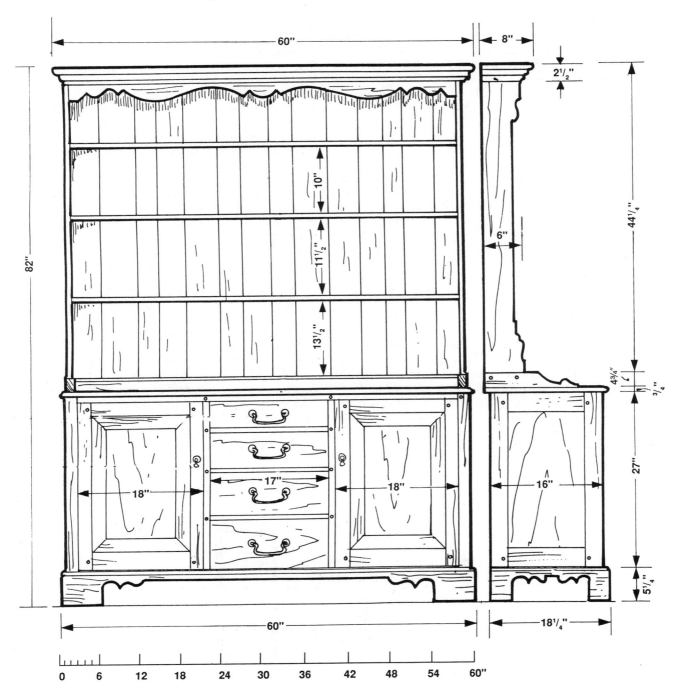

Fig. 11.1. Front and end elevations with main sizes.

31

saw or on the spindle moulder, the sliding table makes an excellent tenoning carriage. The saw is handy when only a couple of rails are involved, as it requires minimal setting; but where quantity, speed, and accuracy matter the spindle is far more efficient.

I cut the rails to length first, and included an allowance for the tenons which were about 1¼in long. The stop was set at a distance equal to the shoulder length plus one tenon length from the maximum projection of the cutting circle. Because of the cutting action of the spindle, it was essential to back up the rail with a piece of scrapwood to avoid spalling. Any haunching was carried out on the saw, working against the rip fence and finished off by removing the waste on the bandsaw.

Having formed a perfect tenon, I needed a mortise of equal accuracy. The K260 machine has a mortising tool which is mounted in a chuck that is an extension of the planer cutter block, and if your machine is similarly fitted it is absolutely essential to guard the cutter block when using the mortiser, because it will still be revolving although it is not needed.

The mortising tool formed rounded ends to the mortises, and these required either that the tenons should be rounded to match, or – more neatly – that the mortises be squared up by hand with a mortise chisel.

PLYWOOD
Just as much old furniture employed second grade timber for groundwork that was later to be veneered, and also for interior work, I used plywood for parts of the construction. Conservation of solid timber provided a good enough reason, but plywood is also an excellent material in its own right for those parts such as cabinet bottoms, backs, divisions, shelves, and drawer bottoms that are seldom seen; the edges can be lipped where necessary.

FIELDED PANELS
An attractive decoration for a panel is fielding, which I employed on the doors; as the end panels were a little narrow for such treatment, I left them plain.

I worked the fielding on the spindle moulder using a Whitehill-type cutter head with a straightforward square cutter angled at about 2 degrees, see Fig. 11.2. Working with the cutter head below the panel, the spindle height could be finely adjusted until I had formed a tongue on the panel that fitted snugly in the groove on the corresponding frame.

This operation used a large cutting circle and therefore a wide opening between the fences, and this is always a possible source of danger. When it is unavoidable, and/or when short pieces are being machined, a cover board or false fence should be used. This is a thin piece of material (¼in ply is ideal) tacked to the existing fences. I ensured minimum cutter projection by actually cutting into the cover board from behind, just above the desired height, and then backing off to give a slight clearance.

When fielding a panel, I found it best to start on the end grain and work clockwise around the panel, so that any spalling when I machined the end grain was removed when I worked the long grain.

The panels were dimensioned so that they were inserted by a depth of ⅜in into each stile or rail, and this allowed for the most severe shrinkage. You must also take care during assembly that no glue accidentally gets into the groove and sticks to the panel to prevent it moving.

ASSEMBLY
The base-cabinet top utilised three pieces to make up the width, and I selected the wood to achieve a matching grain pattern. Each joint had first to be straightened and squared on the surfacer, and it was necessary to hold the boards firmly against the fence with a slow and steady feed for best results. Then I shot each joint by hand planing, and worked a very slight hollow over the length to compensate for movement at the ends. I then cramped up the pieces, using a PVA adhesive, and left them overnight to set.

Because of the width of the top (18¼in), I used the surfacing fence as a guide for ripping, the sliding table again making it easy to finish off to exact dimensions. The moulded detail (Fig. 11.3A) was shaped in two operations on the spindle moulder; the bottom edge was finished off by hand.

The top was finally fixed to the carcase by screwing through the top rails, the kickers, and the odd batten; I remembered to enlarge the screw holes (as in slot-screwing) to allow movement of the timber

The bracket base had an ovolo profile machined on its top edge which was spindled in one operation, and then fixed by gluing and screwing. I cut the mitred corners with the saw blade canted to 45 degrees; by once again using the sliding table, you can get them perfect. You could either shape the base on the bandsaw before fixing it, or afterwards by using a jigsaw – whichever is the easier.

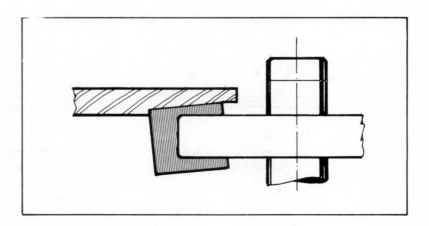

Fig. 11.2. Diagram of fielding with a Whitehill cutter.

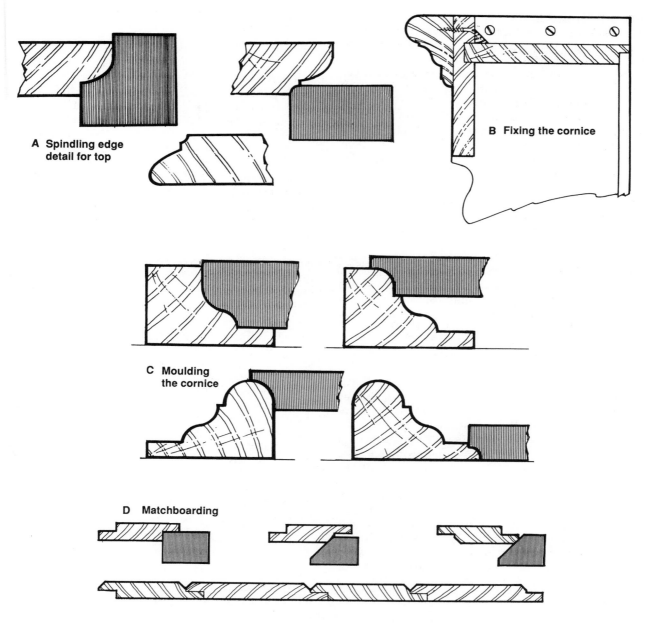

A Spindling edge detail for top

B Fixing the cornice

C Moulding the cornice

D Matchboarding

Fig. 11.3. Methods of spindling mouldings, fixing the cornice (B), and matchboarding (D).

DRAWERS

The drawer construction made a feature of handcut dovetails and one of the secrets of successful dovetailing is careful preparation from the initial choice of wood, through the machining, to gauging the joint accurately.

Drawer slips were used to hold the ¼in ply bottoms in place, and these were easily grooved and rounded on the spindle. The good fitting and working of the drawers depends on the care taken to ensure that the drawer is square, parallel, and of equal width front and back.

HANDLES

I did not want to distract from the mellow appearance of the dresser, so I kept the brass handles simple, with drop handles on the doors and swan-necked ones on the drawers. Much of the brassware sold today is coated with an uninteresting protective lacquer, and I removed this by soaking the handles in cellulose thinners overnight. Then I rubbed the fittings with steel wool to produce an effective dull finish that complemented the colour of the wood.

DRESSER TOP

As the dresser top was a separate unit I was able to make it after the base cupboard was completed. Most of the work involved was in the shaped ends, the feet, and the frieze rail, and these were cut on the bandsaw. I fastened the two ends together with pins so that they could be cut out and cleaned up as one, thus giving a perfect match and a worthwhile time saving.

The horizontal shelves and rails can be fixed by means of housings, tenons, or dowels. On many old dressers, shelves were tenoned right through the ends and wedged; provided this is done neatly, it can be an attractive form of exposed jointing. The shelves had a single bead machined on their front edges, and a plate groove was a useful addition for displaying china etc.

BOARDED BACK

The back of the dresser section was made up of random width V-jointed boards, which were fixed in the rebates with nails.

I selected sufficient wood from ½in stuff to cover the width of the piece. I then ripsawed this, with economy in mind, into random widths varying from 2¼in to 4½in, bearing in mind that ⅜in of board width would be lost in the joint. I planed and thicknessed the boards to about ⅜in thick, and then straightened each edge to provide a starting point for subsequent accurate machine jointing.

Using the spindle moulder with rebating cutters in the head, I then rebated each board on diagonally opposing edges to ⅜in deep and to exactly half its thickness. After choosing and face-marking the best side, the V-bevel was formed in two operations; one side needed more depth to clear the rebates, with a pair of 45 degree cutters in the head; see Fig. 11.3D.

An even balance was desirable among the various widths of board for the back and I took some care to bring this about. Also, I found that polishing of the top section was easier if the back was left out and fitted after final waxing.

CORNICE

Adding a good cornice made all the difference to the overall effect of the design, and for this a length of 3in by 2in stuff was machined down to 2½in by 1¾in, ready for spindling to profile.

This type of moulding had to be machined in several passes, using a different cutter profile for each particular detail; I needed three shapes of cutters, requiring four passes (Fig. 11.3C).

Triangulating the section on the circular saw will reduce the amount of waste to be removed and must improve safety; with heavily shaped pieces of moulding such as this, some planning is essential if you are to arrive at the best sequence of cuts. And, of course, you may even have to supplement the spindle moulder with shaping by hand to produce results.

POLISHING

As chestnut is naturally pale, I gave it some colour and warmth with a light wash of stain (Vandyke brown at about half normal strength). Then I used Jenkins 'pale outside' polish to seal the piece, brushing it on and then cutting it down with wet-and-dry paper. Depth was achieved by padding on a further three or four coats. After leaving these to harden for 24 hours, I dulled the surface with steel wool and then waxed it.

This finish produces a durable result that requires little attention except for an occasional re-waxing, and it brings out the beauty of the grain without obliterating it.

CUTTING LIST

	INCHES			MM		
	L	W	T	L	W	T
Base Cabinet						
4 corner posts	32¾	2¾	1⅝	832	70	41
2 top rails (A)	14½	4¼	¹³⁄₁₆	369	108	21
2 bottom rails (A)	14½	4¼	¹³⁄₁₆	369	108	21
2 panels	21¼	12½	⁹⁄₁₆	540	318	14
1 top	60½	18½	¹³⁄₁₆	1536	470	21
4 rails (B)	57½	2¾	¹³⁄₁₆	1460	70	21
2 divisions (C)	27½	2¾	¹³⁄₁₆	698	70	21
3 drawer rails (C)	18½	2¾	¹³⁄₁₆	470	70	21
1 base	60½	5½	¾	1536	140	19
2 base returns	18½	5½	¾	470	140	19
4 stiles	26½	2	¹³⁄₁₆	673	51	21
2 top rails (A)	17¼	2	¹³⁄₁₆	438	51	21
2 bottom rails (A)	17¼	2¾	¹³⁄₁₆	438	70	21
2 panels	22⅞	15¼	⁹⁄₁₆	581	388	14
1 drawer front	18	4⅝	¹¹⁄₁₆	457	118	18
1 back	18	3¾	⁵⁄₁₆	457	95	8
2 sides	15⅞	4⅝	⁵⁄₁₆	403	118	8
1 drawer front	18	5⅝	¹¹⁄₁₆	457	143	18
1 drawer back	18	4¾	⁵⁄₁₆	457	121	8
2 drawer sides	15⅞	5⅝	⁵⁄₁₆	403	143	8
1 drawer front	18	6⅝	¹¹⁄₁₆	457	168	18
1 drawer back	18	5¾	⁵⁄₁₆	457	146	8
2 drawer sides	15⅞	6⅝	⁵⁄₁₆	403	168	8
1 drawer front	18	7⅝	¹¹⁄₁₆	457	194	18
1 drawer back	18	6¾	⁵⁄₁₆	457	172	8
2 drawer sides	15⅞	7⅝	⁵⁄₁₆	403	194	8
4 drawer bottoms, ply	17⅜	15⅝	¼	442	397	6
1 cabinet bottom, ply	57½	11¾	¾	1460	298	19
2 divisions, ply	27⅜	14¼	¾	695	362	19
1 back, ply	57½	27¼	¼	1460	692	6
Top section						
2 ends (D)	51½	6¼	¹³⁄₁₆	1308	159	21
2 feet	14½	2½	1¹⁄₁₆	369	64	27
3 shelves	56¼	4	¹³⁄₁₆	1428	102	21
1 top	56¼	5¾	¹³⁄₁₆	1428	146	21
1 frieze rail	56¼	5¼	¹³⁄₁₆	1428	133	21
1 bottom rail	56	2½	¹³⁄₁₆	1422	64	21
1 cornice	80½	2¾	1¾	2044	70	45
Back boards to cover	50½	57¼	⅜	1282	1454	10

Notes:– the lengths of items marked (A) include 1¼in (32mm) tenons; the lengths of items marked (B) include 1in (25mm) tenons; the lengths of items marked (C) include ½in (13mm) tenons; the lengths of items marked (D) include 2¼in (58mm) tenons.

Working allowances have been made to lengths and widths; thicknesses are net.

LANCASHIRE-STYLE DRESSER

This project was primarily designed to demonstrate the ability range of a universal woodworking machine and I wish to thank Kity (UK), 6, Acorn Park, Charlestown, Shipley, West Yorks BD17 7SW, for their generous help.

Being a believer in good proportions, I started by consulting a dictionary of 19th and early 20th century furniture. I liked the proportions of a dresser made by Norman and Stacey in 1910, but I felt it was much too fussy in general, so I refined it to what you see here. I left the colour natural, and used a clear melamine catalytic lacquer finish.

GENERAL REMARKS

Having drawn the design up in detail I prepared a cutting list. The rule of thumb when buying sawn hardwood is that the effective yield is around one third of the original rough-sawn volume; this dresser used a fair amount of timber, which in total weighed about 2cwt when it arrived.

One restriction of my universal Kity K5 is the 6in planer width, which meant that planking would be required sometimes but I find this no great disadvantage with a small workshop.

A universal machine provides no short cuts from

conventional cabinet making work, but it enables you to start from rough-sawn timber and end up with flat boards to specific thickness and squareness. To achieve this you need accurate marking out, plus the appropriate selection of grain direction of the timber, and careful and accurate use of the machine during each process.

The finish you get from the planer/thicknesser – however sharp the blades and fine the cut – is not a suitable final finish, and to get perfect surfaces you must plane them by hand with a finely-set plane, followed by scraping with a sharp cabinet scraper, and finally glasspapering with the usual sequence of grades.

Hand trimming is necessary with mortise and tenon joints. The square mortise produced requires finishing by hand, and with tenons it's not safe to try to cut to a marked line; saw crosscuts first to the marked line and then use the machine, leaving, say, 1/16in to be finally hand-trimmed; this takes a little time.

BOTTOM CARCASE

After preparing boards for the two carcase sides, I made them up into panels with loose ply tongues by using the spindle moulder to cut 3/16in grooves in the edges; this meant employing a TCT grooving cutter, slotting from the fair face of each board to produce an almost perfect joint. I had previously trimmed the edges with a shooting plane, because the planer table was too short to give an edge straight enough for a clean joint.

With the other bottom carcase components prepared, I cut 1/2in tenons with the spindle moulder, using the tenoning plate and two TCT cutters ganged up with 1/2in spacers. I used the slot mortiser for the matching holes, squaring them out afterwards by hand.

I had to cut the mortises on the sides of the carcase with a power router, and then I used it to rebate the back edges of the sides of the carcase. Next, I rebated the back edges to the sides, and cut dovetails by hand in the horizontal top pieces and the sides.

Before gluing up I finished all the wood, and identified the different pieces by sticking on small adhesive circles of coloured paper which you can get from any stationer. Then I glued up the whole carcase and cramped it all in one stage; it's a bit arduous if there's only one pair of hands, and it takes a lot of cramps!

TOP CARCASE

After preparing the wood for all the component parts, I made up the sides and base in a similar manner to the bottom side panels, rebating both at the back. I used the spindle moulder again for the tenons, and routed the mortise slots on the sides and base. I find cutting tenons by machine gives me consistent dimensions, so I only have to make a short test-piece tenon as a model for the mortises, and achieve a good tight fit every time. I used no screws except where the verticals were mortised into the base, and these don't show. Then I glued and cramped the top carcase together.

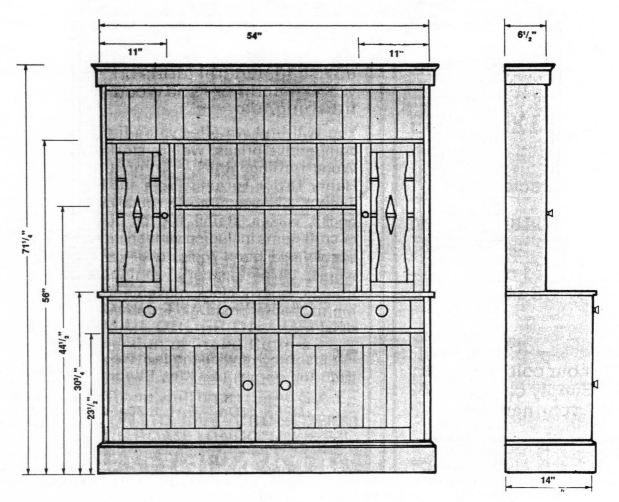

Fig. 12.1. Front and end elevations with principal sizes.

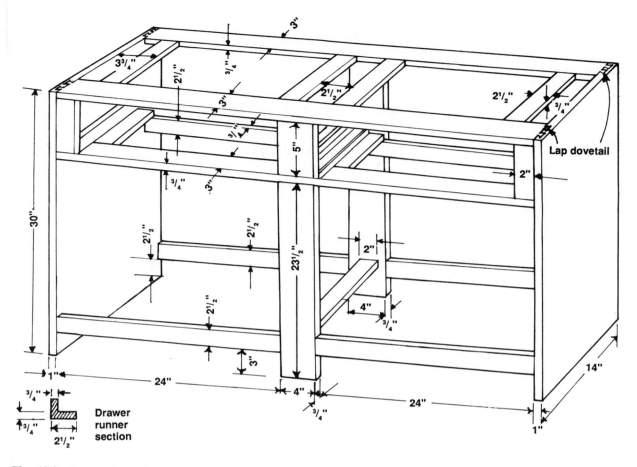

Fig. 12.2. Construction and sizes of bottom carcase.

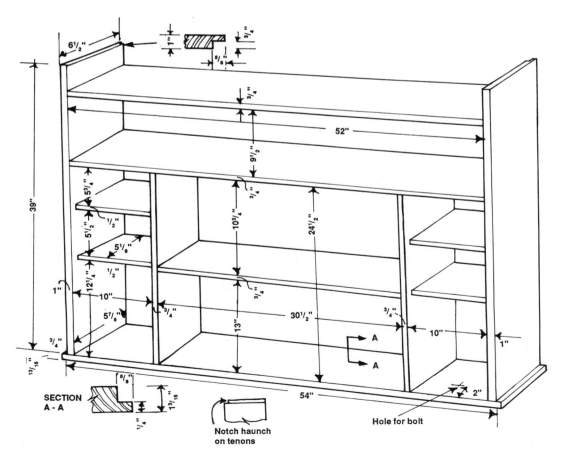

Fig. 12.3 Construction and sizes of upper part.

37

DRESSER TOP

I selected two boards with good grain for this, using loose-tongued joints again. However, I stopped the slots for these 2in from each end, and I had to take care when feeding the leading edges into the slotting cutter on the spindle moulder.

The top is secured by screwing through from the underside of the carcase top, with slotted holes at the front to allow for possible movement.

BACK PLANKING

I used ½in material for this, selecting the boards to get the best effect. I cut tongues and grooves on the spindle moulder with paired ³⁄₁₆in cutters, setting the far edge of the guide 1mm proud of the leading one to allow for the cut taken on the face of the board.

As ash has a tendency to move, allow a ¹⁄₁₆in gap in each joint when screwing the boards centrally to the carcase horizontals.

DRAWERS

I constructed the drawers in the conventional way, with lapped dovetails at the front and through dovetails at the back, cutting them all by hand, and rebated the bottom fronts to accept the ³⁄₁₆in ply bottoms on the spindle moulder.

CUPBOARD DOORS

I shaped the centre panels of the top cupboard doors with a bandsaw, and finished them by hand. After making the slot mortises on the spindle moulder, I squared them up with a mortise chisel.

On the bottom cupboard doors, I worked rebates for the panels, using a ⁵⁄₁₆in TCT grooving cutter; the panels are ½in material, tongued and grooved as for the top back planks. After gluing up the frame, I screwed on the planks, again allowing ¹⁄₁₆in gaps for expansion; I finished the doors by fitting hinges, catches and locks.

TOP FRIEZE AND PLINTH

Deep mitre joints are difficult to cut to look present-able, so I cut and planed them in-situ, and found band cramps invaluable for this kind of job.

MOULDINGS

Before making these on the spindle moulder, I checked the direction of the grain to ensure the best finish I could get. Then I mitred the corners by hand, leaving them overlong to allow for fitting.

ASSEMBLY

Once the drawers were fitted into the carcase, I screwed on the top frieze and bottom plinth from behind, before fitting and gluing the top and bottom mouldings. The bottom cupboard back and floor were sawn by hand from ³⁄₁₆in ply, trimmed to fit and screwed to the carcase. Having fitted the cupboard doors and drilled and recessed holes for bolting the top carcase to the bottom, I turned the cupboard and drawer knobs.

FINISHING

I went over all wood surfaces with a cabinet scraper followed by glasspapering, finishing with 320-grit garnet paper. After damping down to raise the grain, I glasspapered again with worn 320-garnet paper.

Then I lacquered all over, inside and out, using a precatalysed acrylic lacquer diluted 50/50 with thinners (white spirit), applying it with a squirrel-mop type of brush. When this first coat was dry I de-nibbed it with 0000 steel wool, and removed all dust with a tack rag before rubbing over again with worn 320 garnet paper and applying a second coat of thinned lacquer. I de-nibbed this as before when it was thoroughly dry, and left it for a day to harden off. The final coat was in a satin finish lacquer, again diluted 50/50, and when this was dry I de-nibbed it very lightly as with the other coats. I did the whole job out of doors so that the lacquer fumes were soon dispersed.

Finally I applied a coat of best quality wax polish which gave an excellent result, and I re-wax it from time to time.

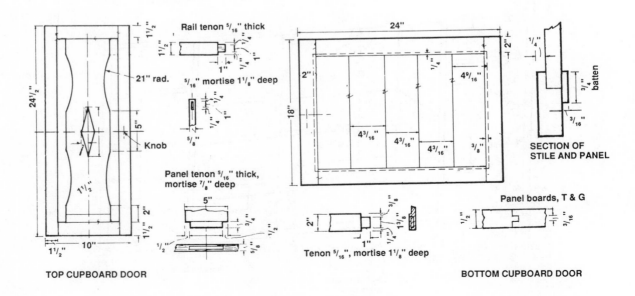

Fig. 12.4. (left) Details of top cupboard door; (right) bottom cupboard door.

CUTTING LIST

	INCHES			MM		
	L	W	T	L	W	T
2 top carcase sides	40	6¾	1	1016	172	25
2 bottom carcase sides	32	14¼	1	813	362	25
1 base plinth front	58	5¼	¾	1473	133	19
2 base plinth ends	16	5¼	¾	406	133	19
1 top front frieze rail	58	4¾	¾	1473	121	19
2 top end frieze rails	16	4¾	¾	406	121	19
11 back boards	38	5½	½	965	140	13
4 top cupboard frame rails	24½	1¾	¾	622	45	19
4 top cupboard frame rails	10	1¾	¾	254	45	19
2 top cupboard panels	24	5¼	½	609	133	13
2 shelves & top verticals	54	6¾	¾	1371	172	19
1 shelf & top vertical	32	6¾	¾	813	172	19
2 shelves & top verticals	28	6¾	¾	711	172	19
10 bottom door panels	16	5¼	½	406	133	13
2 drawer fronts	22	5¼	¾	559	133	19
4 drawer sides	12	5¼	½	305	133	13

CUTTING LIST (continued)

	INCHES			MM		
	L	W	T	L	W	T
2 drawer backs	22	5¼	½	559	133	13
2 front mouldings	58	1¼	¾	1473	32	19
4 end mouldings	16	1¼	¾	406	32	19
4 bottom cupboard frame rails	19	2¼	¾	482	57	19
4 bottom cupboard frame rails	22	2¼	¾	559	57	19
1 dresser table top	58	6¾	15/16	1473	172	24
1 dresser table top	58	7¾	15/16	1473	197	24
1 drawer rail	54	2¾	¾	1371	70	19
4 drawer rails & runners	16	2¾	¾	406	70	19
1 front filling rail	24	4¼	¾	609	108	19
1 front filling rail	6	4¼	¾	153	108	19
2 front filling rails	6	2¼	¾	153	58	19
4 top cupboard shelves	11	5⅜	½	279	137	13

Working allowances have been made to lengths and widths; thicknesses are net.

PITCH PINE DRESSER

I became interested in using pitch pine, with its beautiful grain, when I obtained some old beams from a firm of demolition experts; they cut up the beams into 1in planks and planed them for me. I found the boards varied from 5 to 5¾in wide, so I have avoided giving exact measurements, though if you are buying new timber you could get 5¾in finished boards; see Fig. 13.1 for recommended dimensions.

The dresser is assembled in stages, and I glass-papered all the components for each stage before gluing up as it is easier with the pieces laid flat. I scalloped all facing edges, cupboard doors, etc. with a spokeshave.

BASE SECTION

Start by making up the sides. I sawed lengths off the boards, saving the leftover pieces and marking them so that they could be used for the sides of the top; thus the grain pattern appeared continuous. I cut them slightly oversize to allow a surplus for squaring up the ends along the full width of the joined panels, and I planed each of the four boards for each end to a good square edge, and then joined them using ¾in by ¼in loose tongues. As I have a combination plane I used it to cut the grooves, but they could also be worked with a drunken saw in the sawbench, or a router, or a spindle moulder.

I made up the back of the unit in the same way,

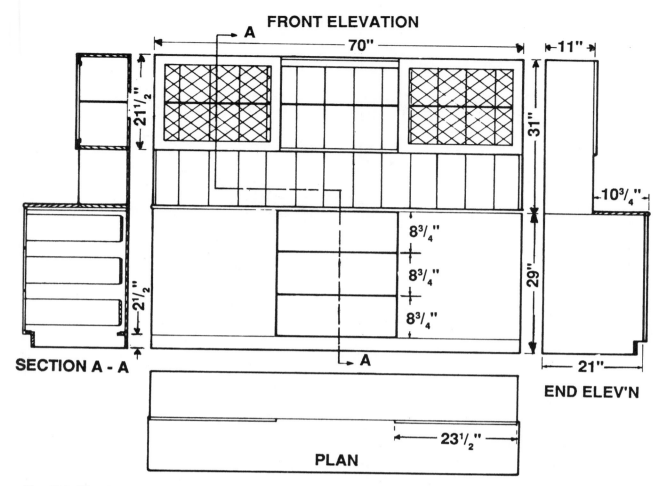

Fig. 13.1. Elevations, plan, and end section with principal sizes.

but applied a ⅛in by ⅛in chamfer along the joining edge of each board; on reflection I realise that ½in ply would be quite suitable, as the back does not show. I glued the back up in three sections (two of four boards, one of five) before finally gluing them together. I planed one long edge of the sides straight and square to act as a datum edge, and marked the top and bottom from this, doing the cutting and planing before finishing the opposite long edge to form a rectangle. I cut a half-thickness rebate at the back, and also cut the recesses at the front bottom corners for the plinth rail.

Then I prepared the division pieces; these were to be butt-jointed to the back. Note that the recess for the plinth rail is higher with these division pieces, since the top horizontal section of the plinth rail, which acts as a front support for the bottom shelves, is butted up to them, while it is dovetailed in at each end.

Then I cut the plinth rail and its bottom front shelf support, cutting the dovetails in the latter. The rear shelf support and four base support rails are rebated ⅛in by ½in for the bottom shelves. I also cut cross rails, making tenons at their ends and mortising them into the base support rails. I half-lapped the rear base support rail to receive the base rails which fit each side of the division pieces.

BASE ASSEMBLY

I started assembling the base by gluing and screwing through the back into the sides, into the top back rail (you could slot-screw here), and into the rear shelf support rail. I offered the division pieces up to the back and marked and cut the cut-outs for the top, the shelf support rails, and the base top front rail. I also marked out and cut mortises for the drawer division rails, and cut tenons on these rails to match.

After gluing and cramping the drawer division rails to the division pieces and checking for squareness, I let this section dry before gluing and screwing it into place, with screws going through the back into the division pieces. I screwed the top back rail sections between the divisions, and the bottom shelf support to the division pieces. Then I glued and screwed the plinth rail to the bottom front shelf support, setting the screws in the rebate so they would be covered by the bottom shelves. I used glue blocks to fasten the plinth rail to the division pieces and the ends.

After gluing and cramping the side base supports and the base cross-rails together, I glued and screwed them into the half-lap cut-outs in the bottom front shelf support. I also glued and screwed the rear base support rails into the ends and the division pieces.

Turning my attention to the top section of the base, I cut dovetails on the ends of the top front rail and the ends; after fastening these together I glued and screwed corner block strengtheners and division piece strengtheners into place.

Then I prepared boards to make up the front top surface of the base, behind which the top section sat. This overlapped the front unit by 1in and the ends by ½in, and was rebated underneath at the back; I glued and screwed it from beneath into position. Then I cut and fitted the bottom shelves, which were ⅛in ply.

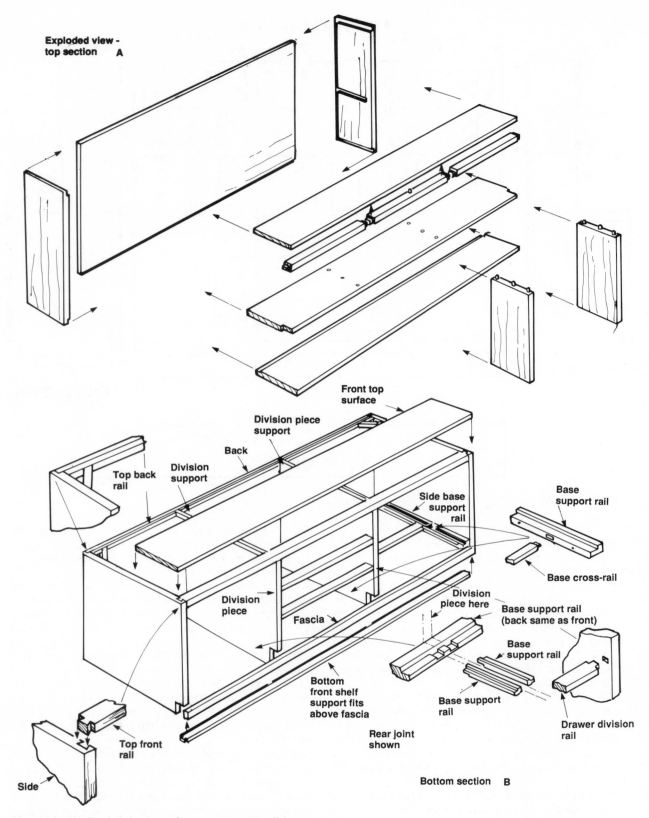

Exploded view - top section A

Front top surface

Division piece support

Back

Division support

Top back rail

Base support rail

Side base support rail

Base cross-rail

Division piece

Fascia

Division piece here

Base support rail (back same as front)

Base support rail

Base support rail

Bottom front shelf support fits above fascia

Rear joint shown

Drawer division rail

Top front rail

Side

Bottom section B

Fig. 13.2. (A) Exploded view of top section; (B) of bottom section.

CUPBOARD DOORS AND DRAWERS

I selected the wood for the doors and drawers carefully before joining the boards together in the same way as I did for the ends. The three drawer fronts can be made up as one, then cut into three pieces so as to get the grain continuous. The drawer backs and sides were comb-jointed; see Fig. 13.5.

To fit the doors, I lined the face edge up with the outer edge of the unit, with a ⅛in gap between the top of the door and the underside of the top front surface. I trimmed the lower edge level with the bottom of the underside plinth rail; the final vertical edge finishes ¹⁄₁₆in to one side of the centre of the division piece.

For the drawer fronts I left the made-up boards in one piece until I had made the drawers, planing one long edge to work from. Once the drawers were completed I cut the fronts, leaving a gap of ⅛in

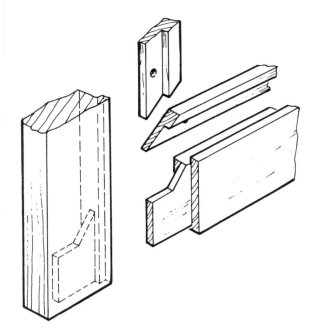

Fig. 13.3. Details of haunched tenons and rebated members in the upper doors, and the mitred beading for the heavy leaded panes.

between each drawer, and ¹⁄₁₆in between the drawer sides and the cupboard doors. The drawers themselves open and close on steel runners; Figs.13.4 and 13.5.

TOP SECTION

I made up panels for the ends, top, division pieces, base, centre shelf, and top back. When the glue had set on the back piece, I planed the bottom edge straight and square, and cut it to the same length as the base back.

The base matches up with the top front surface section, so I planed it to width, and rebated the front edge to match the rebate on the top front surface (screws through the rebates held the sections together later). I then cut the base to the same length as the back.

Next, I planed the ends to the same width as the base of the top, but cut them ⅜in longer than the

back; the bottom edge of this piece rested on the top of the lower end piece and had to be cut exactly to fit. I worked the three rebates on the top and bottom edges and the rear long edge.

Then I planed the division pieces; these were the widths of the ends less the thickness of the back, and were butt-jointed to the back. I prepared the top middle rail, and cut mortises and tenons for the rail, and cut mortises and tenons for the rail and division pieces. The centre shelf was the same width as the division pieces and the same length as the back. Now I prepared the top, and dowelled the division pieces into it and into the centre shelf. Mortise and tenon joints were used for the left and right hand top rails into the division pieces and the ends.

TOP ASSEMBLY (Fig. 13.2)

Having assembled all pieces dry first to see where the cramps had to go, I checked the joints, then dismantled the assembly and had a practice run through, since there were many joints to be put together quickly. I glued up the whole of the top section at one time, except the back, doing it in position on the base, using a sheet of newspaper to protect the base. I checked for squareness as I cramped up, and once the glue was set, I fitted the back.

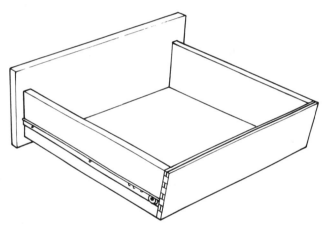

Fig. 13.5. Showing comb joint between drawer side and back; also steel drawer slides.

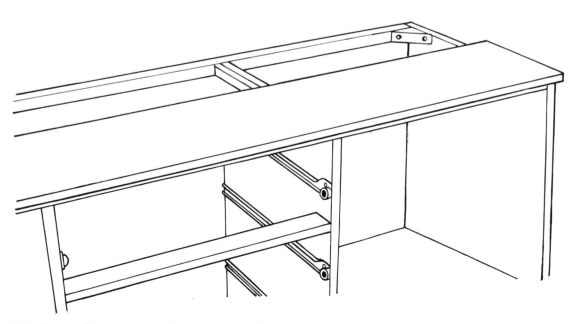

Fig. 13.4. Corner of bottom section showing drawer rails and steel runners.

GLAZED DOORS

Now I was ready to start the frames for these. They were rebated for the glass, with haunched mortise and tenon joints, the glass being fixed by mitred fillets. I finished the doors with ¼in strips of lead, applied diagonally, starting from the centre and working out both ways. The inner shelves were also made of glass, with the front edges ground off for safety.

Having used my orbital sander at each stage of assembly, I now glasspapered with a sequence of grades, finishing with flour paper. I stained with a mixture of two parts mahogany to one part dark oak, followed by applications of high gloss polyurethane lacquer. Although I used recovered pitch pine, the dresser could easily be made from new pine or a hardwood.

CUTTING LIST

	INCHES			MM		
	L	W	T	L	W	T
Base						
1 back	70½	29¼	¾	1790	740	19
2 sides	29½	21¼	¾	749	540	19
1 top surface	71½	11	¾	1816	279	19
2 divisions	20¼	25	¾	514	635	19
2 doors	23½	26¼	¾	597	667	19
1 plinth front	70½	3¼	¾	1790	83	19
1 front shelf support	70½	2¾	¾	1790	70	19
1 back shelf support	69	1½	1	1752	38	25
4 side shelf supports	20¾	1½	1	527	38	25
1 top front rail	69¾	2¼	¾	1771	58	19
1 top back rail	69	1½	1	1752	38	25

CUTTING LIST (continued)

	INCHES			MM		
	L	W	T	L	W	T
1 corner support	36½	1½	1	927	38	25
2 shelf support cross rails	22½	1½	⅞	571	38	22
2 drawer division rails	25½	2¼	¾	648	58	19
3 drawer fronts	24	9	¾	610	229	19
6 drawer sides	19½	6¼	¾	495	159	19
3 drawer backs	24	6	¾	610	153	19
3 drawer bottoms, ply	24	19¼	⅛	610	489	3
6 base rails	24	⅞	⅝	610	22	16
2 bottom shelves, ply	19½	22¾	⅛	495	578	3
2 internal shelves	17½	22¾	¾	444	578	19
Top						
1 back	70½	31¼	¾	1790	793	19
2 sides	31½	11¼	¾	800	286	19
1 top	70½	11¼	¾	1790	286	19
1 base	70¼	11¼	¾	1784	286	19
2 divisions	20½	10½	¾	521	267	19
3 cornice pieces	24½	2	¾	623	51	19
1 centre shelf	70¼	10½	¾	1784	267	19
4 door frame rails	24	2¾	¾	610	70	19
4 door frame rails	22	2¾	¾	558	70	19
8 fillets	21½	1	⅝	546	25	16

Working allowances have been made to lengths and widths; thicknesses are net.

DRESSER WITH GLAZED CUPBOARDS

The dresser is familiar to all. This unusual and interesting piece, however, comes from Ireland, where it was made (as far as I can discover) at the turn of the century. It has now found a home in Lancashire.

Made of pine, it has clearly been stripped at some time, and its present finish consists of matt polyurethane lacquer and wax. The base and upper units are completely separate, fitting together with the aid of dry dowel pegs for location. All constructional techniques are traditional – though there is, of course, plenty of scope for modification according to individual taste, skills, and equipment.

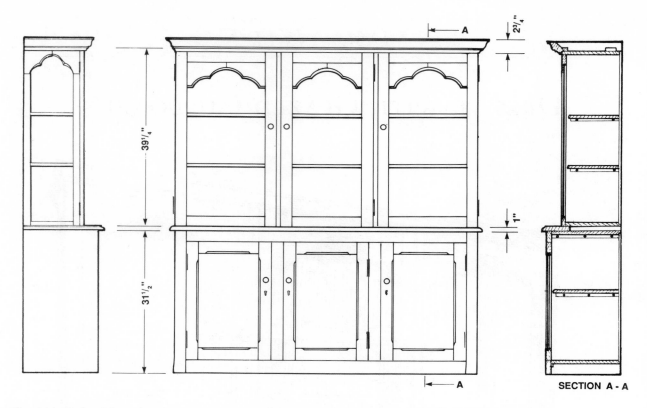

Fig. 14.1. End and front elevations, and section on end. Principal dimensions are shown. The shaped gussets on the doors are simply butted and glued to the inner edges of the frames.

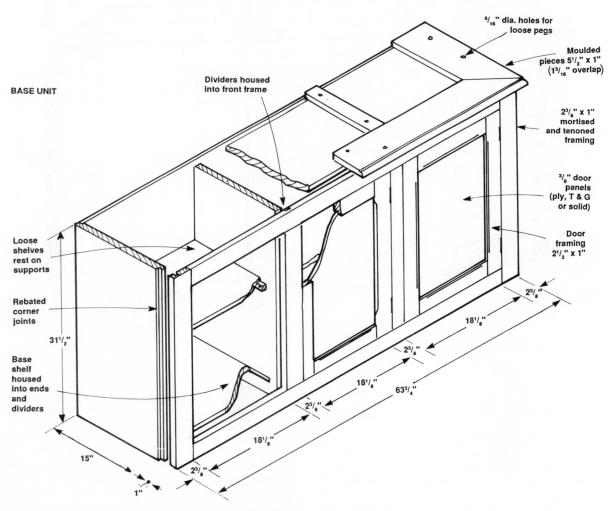

Fig. 14.2. Constructional details and dimensions of base unit.

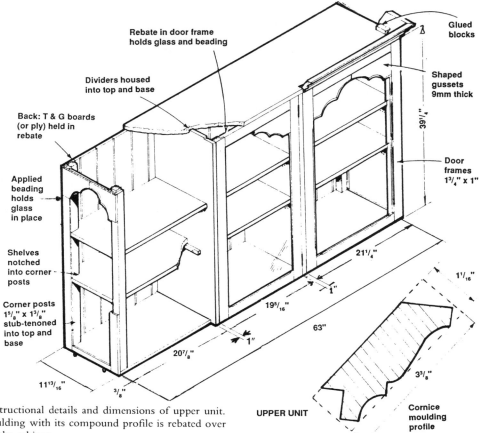

Rebate in door frame
holds glass and beading

Dividers housed
into top and base

Back: T & G boards
(or ply) held in
rebate

Applied
beading
holds
glass
in place

Shelves
notched
into corner
posts

Corner posts
1⁵/₈" x 1³/₈"
stub-tenoned
into top and
base

Glued
blocks

Shaped
gussets
9mm thick

Door
frames
1³/₄" x 1"

39¹/₄"

21¹/₄"

19⁵/₁₆"

63"

1"

1"

20⁷/₈"

11¹³/₁₆"

³/₈"

UPPER UNIT

1¹/₁₆"

3³/₈"

Cornice
moulding
profile

Fig. 14.3. Constructional details and dimensions of upper unit. The cornice moulding with its compound profile is rebated over the top panel of the cabinet.

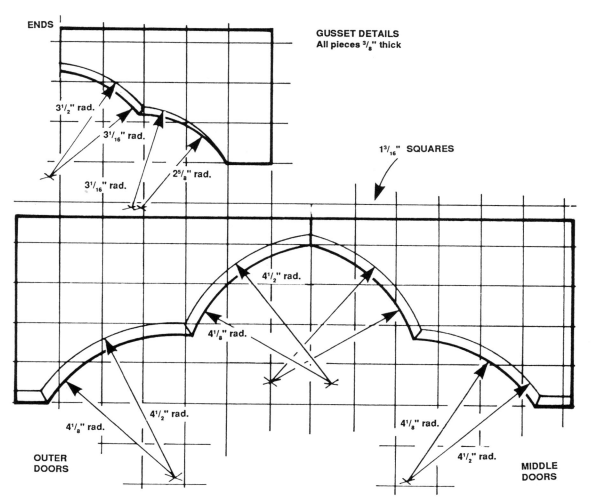

ENDS

GUSSET DETAILS
All pieces ³/₈" thick

3¹/₂" rad.

3¹/₁₆" rad.

3¹/₁₆" rad.

2⁵/₈" rad.

1³/₁₆" SQUARES

4¹/₂" rad.

4¹/₈" rad.

4¹/₂" rad.

4¹/₈" rad.

4¹/₈" rad.

4¹/₂" rad.

OUTER
DOORS

MIDDLE
DOORS

Fig. 14.4. Grid drawing of shaped parts.

CUTTING LIST

	INCHES			MM		
	L	W	T	L	W	T
Base unit carcase						
4 ends & dividers	31	15¾	1	788	400	25
6 shelves	22	15	1	558	381	25
1 top	64	15	11	1625	381	25
2 front frame rails	64	2⅜	1	1625	60	25
4 front frame rails	31	2⅜	1	788	60	25
6 shelf supports	14	¾	½	355	19	13
1 back, ply or t&g boards	64	30	⅜	1625	762	10
1 moulded piece	67	5½	1	1701	140	25
2 moulded pieces	18	5½	1	458	140	25
2 spacers	12	2	1	305	51	25
Doors						
6 frame rails	26½	2⅝	1	673	67	25
6 frame rails	18	2⅝	1	458	67	25
3 panels, ply, t&g, or solid	24	15	⅜	610	381	10
Upper unit carcase						
4 corner posts	40	1⅝	1⅜	1016	41	35
2 vertical dividers	40	14	1	1016	356	25
2 top and base panels	64	12	1	1625	305	25
6 shelves	21	12	1	533	305	25
12 shelf supports	12	¾	½	305	19	13
1 back, ply or t&g boards	64	40	⅜	1625	1016	10
Doors						
6 frame rails	40	1¾	1	1016	45	25
6 frame rails	21¼	1¾	1	540	45	25
6 gussets from	65	6	⅜	1651	153	10
5 beadings from	31½	1⅝	⅜	800	41	10
1 moulding	100	3⅜	1⅛	2540	86	29

Working allowances have been made to lengths and widths; thicknesses are net.

MODERN DRESSER WITH SWIVELLING TV TABLE

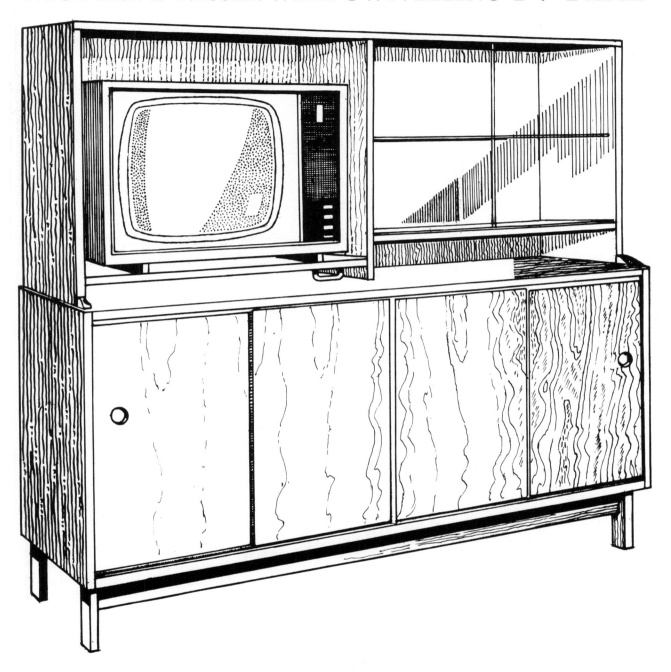

The main virtue of ready-veneered chipboard, of which this dresser was constructed, is that the boards are veneered on both faces and all four edges. Obviously, to take advantage of this, any design made from it must utilise standard sizes and entail as little cutting as possible.

The feature which has decided the shape of the dresser, and its depth from front to back, is the television set. Below that is a drinks cupboard with a light which switches on when the sliding door is opened, and to the right of that another cupboard. On the same level as the TV set is a display cabinet for ceramics or china; and underneath this is a space for magazines.

The main disadvantage of any sort of chipboard is that normal cabinetmaking joints cannot be cut with any degree of strength and accuracy. In the case of the chipboard used here, the strength is, to a large extent, in the facing veneers, and if these are cut through excessively the board loses much of its normal rigidity. The type of construction shown should give a robust and attractive result, bearing in mind this defect.

As a general note, if you have to cut some of the

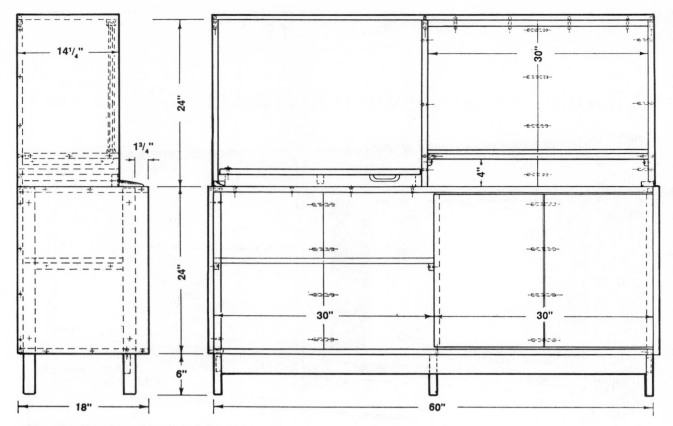

Fig. 15.1. Elevations with principal dimensions.

boards (as is necessary in some parts of the design) obviously it's a good idea to arrange the sawn edges at the back to save re-veneering, except in the case of the television shelf, when one end also needs to be re-veneered.

LOWER UNIT

You will need to notch the two long boards which form the top and bottom of the lower part of the dresser twice at each end. You will also need to notch the legs in the appropriate places on one face to a depth of ⅛in; the front legs are also notched on the front edges ⅛in deep to support the front edges of the chipboard. When assembling, glue and screw the legs into the notches in the boards, and to prevent the lower board sagging you should dovetail a long rail into the backs of the front legs, marking the dovetails out in a trial assembly before gluing up. Also, let a centre leg into the middle of the long rail from the back (see Fig. 15.3).

The construction of the back helps to increase the rigidity of the lower dresser unit, and the back of the right hand cupboard is hardboard or ply on fillets. The back of the drinks cupboard, however, is made of two 15in boards dowelled and glued together. Glue and screw this through the long boards at top and bottom, and also screw it through into the back edge of the back leg.

This is the reason for the back legs being set forward slightly (the thickness of the chipboard is a nominal ¾in, or more exactly, ¹¹⁄₁₆in), and you can conveniently use this setting forward to accommodate a skirting board, if there is one. Between the two lower cupboards put in a partition dowelled into the top of the carcase at the front (screw it in the middle and at the back where the fixing is hidden by the top unit), and also screw it from underneath. It is best to

glue and screw the partition to the two boards of the back as the first step, fixing them in position and then putting on the legs.

DOWELLING

The strength and success of the construction depend very largely on the accuracy of the dowelling. The dowels are ⅜in dia throughout, and it is imperative to use a jig for drilling the holes, locating it in the appropriate position and holding it with a G-cramp. The jig itself is made of hardwood as illustrated in Fig. 15.2; and, if one side is made removable, it can be used for drilling both the ends and faces of the boards.

The jig must obviously be completely accurate and as deep as is practicable. The ⅜in dia hole should, if possible, be drilled through on a vertical drill stand; and if the hole in the jig is equidistant from both ends, it will simplify measuring from either the front or the back edge of the board. The exploded drawing Fig. 15.3, makes clear how the dowels are positioned in the construction.

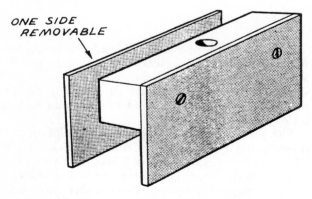

Fig. 15.2. Jig for drilling dowel holes.

50

In a case where you have to dowel two boards together at the edges, you will achieve a more accurate joint if you shoot the two edges first with a plane, checking that the edges are true with a try-square and a straightedge.

You may need to plane away parts of the edge veneer completely. In the case of the two sliding doors, you will find it essential to shoot the appropriate edges of the doors to be joined – obviously if the boards do not join perfectly the sliding door arrangement will not be possible.

When dowelling the boards for the doors you can introduce ⅛in thick strips of a contrasting wood such as ramin between the boards, giving the effect of decorative inlays. Leave the strips standing proud and scrape them flush once the adhesive has set.

THE TOP UNIT

You can see the construction of this in the exploded drawing. Note that the compartment for the TV has no back so that it is well ventilated. The back of the china cabinet comprises two boards dowelled together in the same way as the lower unit. An ebonised support frame beneath the TV takes its weight, which rests on a board that is cut to shape and re-veneered at the edges, see Fig. 15.4. This board is pivoted at the left-hand front corner and you can adjust the viewing angle of the TV by means of the handle on the right.

TELEVISION SUPPORT FRAME

Make this of 1¾in by ⅞in hardwood, lap-dovetailing it at the corners and fixing a central bearer 1⅜in by

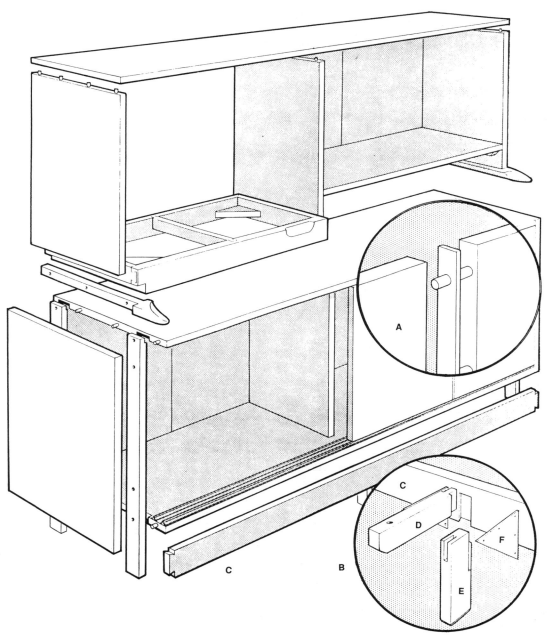

Fig. 15.3. Exploded view of construction. Inset (A) shows method of making door from two boards dowelled together with a thin strip of wood of contrasting colour between; this gives the effect of an inlaid line. Inset (B) shows construction of centre leg. The leg (E) is dovetailed from below into the back of rail (C). Cross piece (D) is tenoned into top of the leg and the construction strengthened by two triangular pieces of ply glued and screwed on. The cross piece (D) is screwed up into dresser bottom. The long rail (C) in the large drawing is shown in front of the legs for clarity.

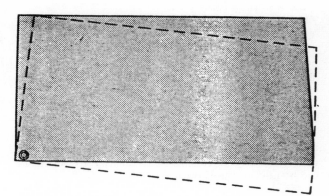

Fig. 15.4. Pivoting the TV table. The shape of the end curve determines how much the table can be pivoted. Obviously the table must not come too far forward or the weight of the set will not be adequately supported.

⅞in, dovetailed in from the top. Cut away the left side of the frame to take a piece of wood which you can shape decoratively at the front, cutting it away to accept the end board and then gluing and screwing the two together – there is a matching piece at the other end of the dresser.

CHINA DISPLAY COMPARTMENT

The bottom of this (4in above the lower unit) is dowelled into the end board and the partition, but you should also fix in two bearers so that the dowels alone do not take the weight; the shelf is also fixed from the cabinet back. You can introduce a ¼in armoured plate glass shelf on bearers, or on movable supports so that the shelf can be raised or lowered. The two ³⁄₁₆in thick glass doors slide in grooved tracks which are glued in.

SLIDING DOOR TRACKS

There are several proprietary patterns which you can buy, but in my design they are in black plastic, ¼in wide by ¼in deep. They are nailed in place with veneer pins, and two small jigs had to be made to space them from the front edge. The gliders that run in the tracks are also plastic and are inserted into the door edges.

To insert the gliders means cutting small mortises into the door edges and you will need to cramp some strips of scrapwood tightly against the edges of the doors to prevent them breaking away when cutting the mortises. Use a sharp craft knife to cut through the edge veneer and down the mortise sides before chiselling out the waste as it is difficult and tricky to chop out the mortises in the normal fashion.

FINISHING

If you want to ebonise the feet, bottom rail, television shelf, and the wood tracks for the glass sliding doors, do it before assembly.

The remainder of the dresser may be stained to whatever colour is desired. In my design an oak stain was used, any excess stain being wiped off immediately. The surfaces were then sealed with clear French polish before filling the grain.

The only difficulty you are likely to meet in staining is with the doors, as it is all too easy to stain or smudge the decorative white strip let in the centre of each door. You can use a steel straightedge and stain up to that, or mask the white wood strip with masking tape. Teak oil was the finish in my design and although its use was a little unorthodox the result was completely satisfactory. The raw back edges of the boards were sealed with a matching wood filler.

Fix the top unit to the lower by screwing from underneath; the top unit can overlap slightly the line of the join between the long top board and end boards of the lower unit – not absolutely necessary, but it does improve the appearance. You will have to reduce the long boards of the bottom unit about ¼in in length before assembly to achieve the effect.

Two handles are needed for the sliding doors and also a handle for the TV shelf; the latter is made out of sheet brass, polished and lacquered, while the shelf pivot is a brass screw and screwcup.

CUTTING LIST

	INCHES			MM		
	L	W	T	L	W	T
Lower unit★						
2 top & bottom pieces, each	60	18	¾	1524	457	19
1 piece for 2 ends	48	18	¾	1219	457	19
1 back	48	15	¾	1219	381	19
2 doors, each	48	15	¾	1219	381	19
1 piece for 2 shelves	60	15	¾	1524	381	19
1 piece for partitions for upper & lower unit	48	15	¾	1219	381	19
Lower unit★★						
4 legs, each	30½	2	⅞	775	51	22
1 front rail	60	3	⅞	1524	76	22
1 piece for 4 shelf bearers	50	1	¾	1270	25	19
1 centre leg	12	2	⅞	305	51	22
1 piece white wood for door strips	49	1	⅛	1244	25	3
Upper unit★						
1 top	60	15	¾	1524	381	19
1 piece for 2 shelves	60	15	¾	1524	381	19
1 piece for 2 ends	60	15	¾	1524	381	19
Upper unit★★						
1 piece for TV shelf frame	88	1⅞	⅞	2234	48	22
1 TV shelf bearer	14	1½	⅞	356	38	22
1 piece for 2 shelf bearers	26	⅞	½	660	22	13
1 cabinet door upper track	31	1	1	787	25	25
1 cabinet door lower track	31	1	½	787	25	13
1 piece for 2 shaped ends	36	2	⅞	914	51	22

Note:– items marked ★ are in particle board: those marked ★★ are in hardwood.
Working allowances have been made to lengths and widths; thicknesses are net.

A PACK-FLAT TABLE

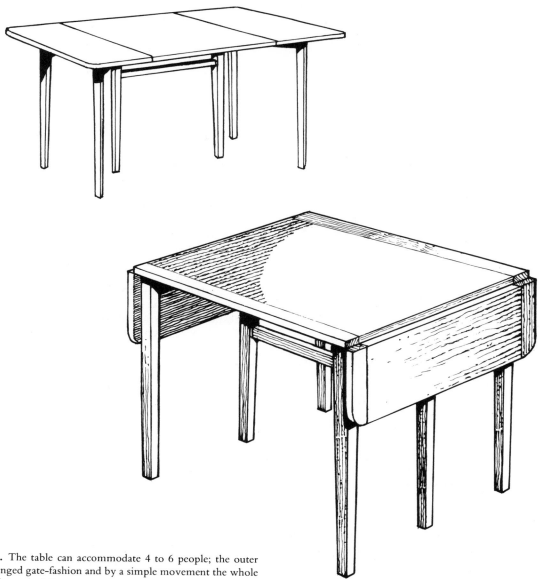

Fig. 16.1. The table can accommodate 4 to 6 people; the outer legs are hinged gate-fashion and by a simple movement the whole table can be packed flat.

Strongly recommended for a small room, this design packs down flat if required and extends to seat six people. Any wood can be used providing it is clean and straightgrained; the top and flaps could be made from a laminated board, blockboard, or plywood with the edges lipped all round in each case.

THE LEGS
Prepare these from 2in squares to finish as thick as possible; taper them to 1¼in at the foot after mortising them for the rails. Note that the tapering commences below the rails.

FIXED AND GATE-LEGS
The two fixed centre legs, A, Fig. 16.3, are connected by the two rails B and C with 1½in long tenons which fit centrally into the legs; you could round off the top edge of lower rail, C, if you wish.

Each gateleg has one rail strongly tenoned to it at the top, but you must keep the top edge of the rail down from the top of the leg to clear the knuckles of the flap hinges, Figs. 16.3 and 16.4. Cut and square off each rail to a length that will allow the legs to close easily at the centre when hinged to the fixed centre legs.

Use good quality strong back flap hinges or, alternatively, brass butt hinges with one wide leaf; screw one leaf to the fixed centre leg A, fixing the other leaf through the gateleg rails with countersunk head bolts of a gauge that will enter the hinge holes, which could be slightly enlarged to suit any bolts you may already have, Fig. 16.4.

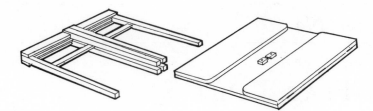

Fig. 16.2. How the table is dismantled and packed flat.

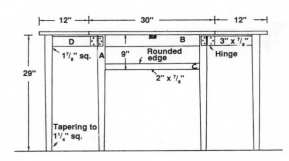

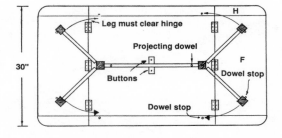

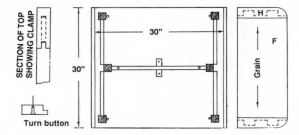

Fig. 16.3. Elevations and plans – bottom plan with flap down.

FLAPS

You will see from Fig. 16.3 that the top and the flaps are solid wood about ⅞in thick, and clamped at each end. They are hinged together with three 2½in brass hinges to each joint.

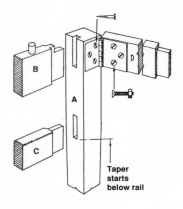

Fig. 16.4. Joints and hingeing detail.

Recess the hinges into the top and the flaps so that you get a close joint when the flaps are down – the outer hinges must be positioned so that the gatelegs clear the knuckles upon closing (Figs. 16.3).

Position the top to the centre legs by fixing two dowels to project from the top of rail B, boring corresponding holes to accept them into the underside of the top. The top is held in position by two turn buttons screwed to it and engaging the rail B, Fig. 16.3, at the centre.

You will need dowel stops for the gatelegs in the positions indicated on the plan, Fig. 16.3. The flaps close upon the main top like a book, and as the dowel stops would prevent this, you will have to bore corresponding holes into the underside for the dowels to enter when the table is packed flat.

CUTTING LIST

	INCHES			MM		
	L	W	T	L	W	T
A 6 legs	29½	2⅛	1⅞	749	54	48
B 1 rail	26	3¾	⅞	660	95	22
C 1 rail	26	2¼	⅞	660	58	22
D 4 hinged rails	13½	3¼	⅞	343	83	22
E 1 top	30½	30¼	⅞	775	769	22
F 2 flaps	30½	12¼	⅞	775	311	22
G 2 clamps	30½	2¾	⅞	775	70	22
H 4 clamps	12½	2¾	⅞	318	70	22

Working allowances have been made to lengths and widths; thicknesses are net.

SNACK STAND

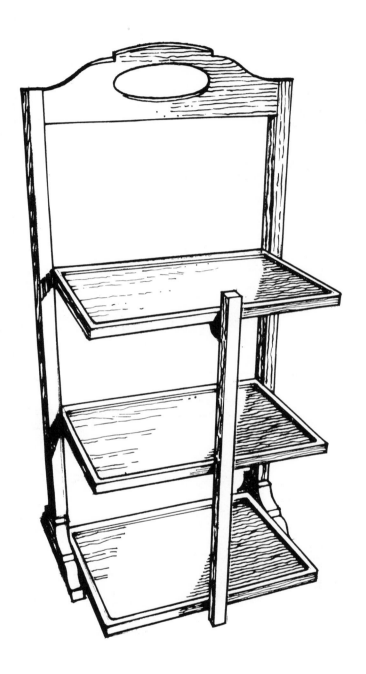

Yes, it does look rather like a cake stand. That's because I adopted the same principle, but I made the supporting surfaces large enough to hold the paraphernalia for afternoon tea or a TV dinner.

You could make the trays from veneered plywood, with beading around the edges. I had some solid oak of suitable size, so I routed out a ³/₁₆in deep recess and thus formed solid wood trays, which I finished with a gouge to create a non-slip surface.

I used dowels to hinge the trays to the uprights,

you have to make sure the holes in the uprights are correctly positioned and of suitable depth for the dowels. I mortised and tenoned the top and bottom to the side uprights, reinforcing the joints with ¼in dowels, as the joints were liable to be subjected to a fair amount of strain. I shaped the edges with a router, but you could chamfer them.

Some areas are going to be difficult to stain if you leave them until after gluing up, so I suggest you stain beforehand. The gluing up is all done at once,

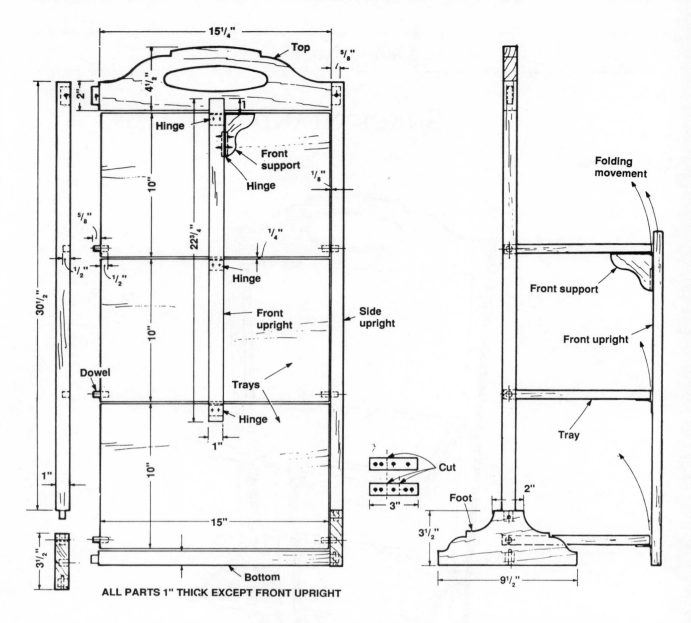

ALL PARTS 1" THICK EXCEPT FRONT UPRIGHT

apart from the feet. Apply candlewax to the dowels on the trap trays so they remain movable.

For the front supports I used 3in brass hinges, sawn as shown. The steel pins slipped out, but I countersank the brass, replaced the pins and burred over their ends with a nail punch. Then I added further countersunk holes as shown.

I racked my brains trying to think of a suitable method of holding the trays in the stacked position, and my final solution was a simple button.

The whole stand is simple . . . but useful too.

CUTTING LIST

	INCHES			MM		
	L	W	T	L	W	T
2 side posts	31½	1¼	1	800	32	25
1 handle	17	4¾	1	432	121	25
1 front upright	23¼	1	¾	590	25	19
2 feet	10	3¾	1	254	95	25
1 cross rail	17	1¼	1	432	32	25
3 trays, each	15½	10¼	⅝	394	260	16
1 front support	3½	3¼	¾	89	83	19

Working allowances have been made to lengths and widths; thicknesses are net.

FOOD PREPARATION WAGON

This design is a useful and attractive addition to the kitchen and as it is fully mobile, you can easily take it into the garden, conservatory, or dining room. Built entirely of oak, its main features are a convenient worktop, three storage drawers for utensils (which can be opened from either side) and a pull-out tray beneath. Four sections of brass-coloured metal tubing prevent large items from sliding off the bottom shelf, and serve as handy towel rails.

CONSTRUCTION – TOP FRAME
Start by cutting the four legs to length from 1½in square material, allowing an extra ¾in at the top for the tenon. Cut the two top end rails from 2in by 1½in timber, again allowing extra length so that you

can safely cut the mortises without the risk of splitting at the ends.

Mark in the position of the mortises on the undersides of both rails to receive the leg tenons. For this, set the mortise gauge to½in between its two points, adjusting the fence so that they mark the wood centrally. Each mortise is then set in by ⅛in from its inside edge and ⅜in from the outside.

Cut all four mortises to a depth of ¾in. Mark out a corresponding tenon at the top of each leg, saw off the waste and trim the four shoulders of each tenon until the joint fits perfectly (Fig. 18.2).

Cut the two top rails from the same 2in by 1½in material, allowing extra length for the tenons at each end.

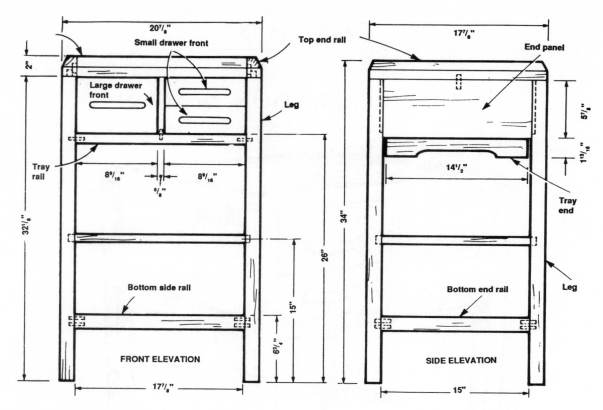

Fig. 18.1. Front and side elevations.

Taking the board for the top shelf, accurately measure its thickness (it should be 13mm, but if you are using veneered ply it might be a fraction more) and set the points of the mortise gauge to this measurement. Adjust the fence to ¼in from the nearest point, and mark in the groove that runs along the inside face of each top rail. These four housing grooves accept the top shelf, Figs. 18.2.

Work the grooves with a power router and a 13mm cutter or you could use a plough plane, with the cutter set to ⅜in deep. The two top side rails need the groove cut along their entire length, but the grooves in the two end rails have to be stopped 1⅛in from each end (Fig. 18.2). This is why the power router, being more accurate to control for a stopped groove, is the best tool for the job. You then only need to square off the rounded ends of the groove with a chisel.

The upper halves of the outside faces of all four rails are chamfered to add to the appearance. Mark the areas of waste first with a marking gauge; score a line halfway down the outside face, and set a line in by one-third of the thickness along the top edge. Cramp each piece firmly in a vice and plane off the waste.

The two end rails are attached to the two side rails with mortise and tenon joints, the mortises being cut in the end rails and the tenons in the sides, Fig. 18.2. A depth of ⅜in is recommended for each joint – as a greater depth could incur the risk of cutting into and weakening the leg joints. If ⅜in seems rather shallow, bear in mind that these joints are further strengthened by the top shelf, which is dowel-jointed into its four grooves.

Trim the four joints so that the rails fit neatly together to make a frame for the top shelf. Mark in the sloped contour of both side rails against the two end rails where they have already been chamfered,

and trim the end rails to their final length, matching the sloped face of the chamfer in the process.

Lightly chamfer the inside top edges of all four rails, working the bevel along the full length of the side rails, and stopping it short on the end rails where it coincides with the chamfering of the side rails. The end rail chamfering is best done with a spokeshave, and cleaned up with a sharp chisel to ensure that the bevels meet perfectly at the rail joints.

Check that the top shelf fits fully into its housing grooves, and tap the rail joints gently together, as a test to satisfy you that the components make a good assembly. For greater strength, the top shelf is dowel-jointed to the rails; drill a single dowel hole at the centre of each groove, and a corresponding hole dead-centre in each of the shelf's four edges; use a ¼in dia centre bit to a depth of ½in.

Cut four 1in long pieces of ¼in dowel, and apply glue into the dowel joints, the grooves (if you are using ply), and the mortise and tenon joints. If you use solid wood for the top, don't apply glue to the grooves or one end of the dowels. Tap the assembly together and cramp it firmly while the glue sets.

LEG FRAMES

Fit the two top end panels to the legs with mortise and tenon joints (Fig. 18.3). Each panel is ⅝in thick, and mounted flush with the inside face of its two supporting legs. Each mortise is ¼in wide and located ½in up from the bottom edge of the panel. The corresponding tenon is marked centrally along both ends of the panel. Cut out the mortises with the router, using a ¼in cutter set to ¼in deep. Stop the router at the point where the mortises end, and square off the end with a chisel.

Mark the tenons on the panels, using the same gauge setting, and remembering the ½in haunch at the bottom (Fig. 18.3), cut the tenons and test them

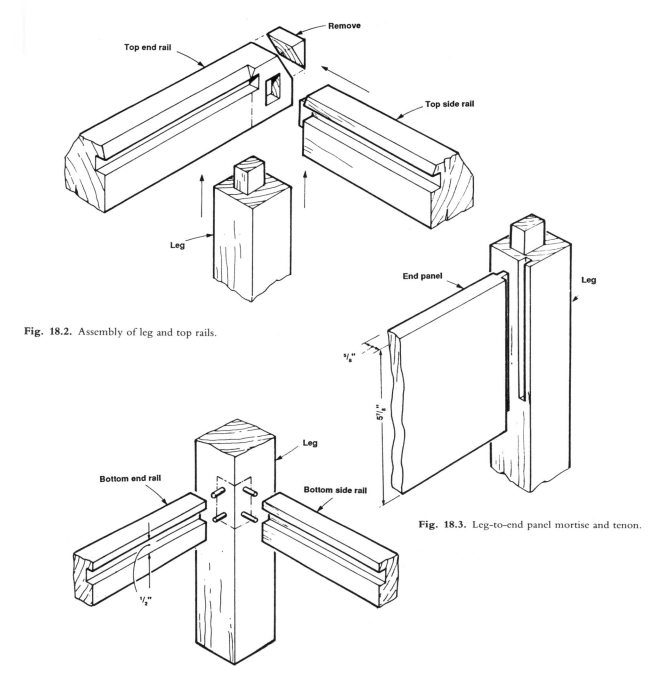

Fig. 18.2. Assembly of leg and top rails.

Fig. 18.3. Leg-to-end panel mortise and tenon.

Fig. 18.4. Dowel joints; leg-to-bottom.

for fit in the long leg mortises. Drill a single ¼in dowel hole in the exact centre of each panel, ½in deep.

Mark the positions of the 'brass' rails – ¾in if you have ¾in tube – in all four legs. This tube is not actually brass on the design illustrated, but a bright-finished metal; you could use brass plated ones. Set the holes slightly off centre to the inside edges, and drill them out ½in deep with a flat bit or a Forstner bit.

Mark for the four bottom rails, which are dowel-led to the legs with two dowels at each end as shown in Fig. 18.4. Cut the four bottom rails slightly oversize, and mark and cut the grooves for the shelf in the same way as you did for the top rails – as wide as the shelf is thick, set ¼in down from the top edge, and ⅜in deep. Cut the rails to exact length and mark and drill accurately for the dowel holes in each end;

before you drill, make sure you also have the positions marked exactly in the legs. A template the size of the rail end section would be useful here to marry the holes in the legs and rails; now you can drill the dowel holes in the legs.

Cut and prepare 16 dowels each 1in long, and glue them into the rail ends. Allow a day for the glue to set hard. Cut the brass tube to length, allowing it to enter ⅜in into each hole, and file off any burrs on the ends.

Cramp each of the four legs vertically in the vice one at a time, bottom end uppermost, and drill a ⅜in hole in the centre of the base to a depth of 1½in. Fit the cylindrical sockets that house the castor wheels you have chosen, tapping them down with a mallet until the serrated shoulder grips the wood.

Mark in the position of the two tray rails on each leg – use another template, perhaps – and drill a

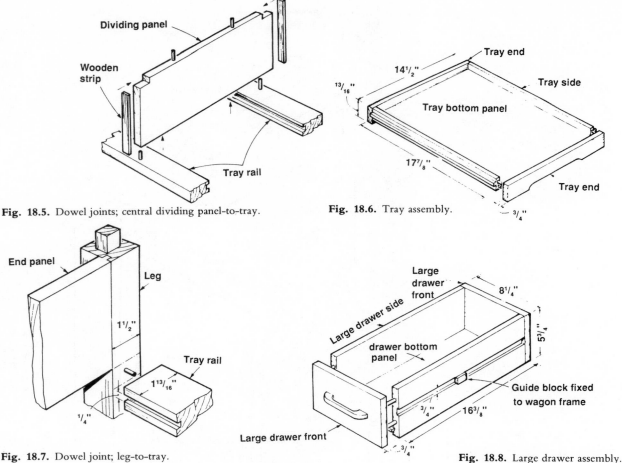

Fig. 18.5. Dowel joints; central dividing panel-to-tray.

Fig. 18.6. Tray assembly.

Fig. 18.7. Dowel joint; leg-to-tray.

Fig. 18.8. Large drawer assembly.

single ¼in dowel hole, ⅜in deep (Fig. 18.7). Assemble the two ends remembering to fit the 'brass' rails, gluing the joints together and cramping up.

DIVIDER, TRAY RAILS, AND ASSEMBLY
Cut the dividing panel that separates the drawers from one another to the same depth as the two end panels, notching it to fit round the top side rails and butt up against the underside of the top shelf assembly (Fig. 18.5). The ends of this dividing panel do not lie flush with the outer faces of the top side rails or the tray rails; they stop ³⁄₁₆in short, leaving room to fit narrow strips of oak which cover the otherwise exposed end grain.

Drill two dowel holes of ¼in dia to joint the dividing panel to the underside of the top shelf, and mark and drill the shelf as well; the divider is also dowelled to the tray rails, so drill for those dowels now. Then glue two short dowels in place in the top edge and fit the panel in position under the shelf.

Uncramp the two end assemblies, and temporarily fit the leg tenons into their mortises in the top shelf frame assembly. This will give you the accurate length for the two tray rails. Cut these rails from 1¾in by 1in material, marking in a groove along the 1in thick edge to accept the tongues of the tray. Mark the grooves with the mortise gauge, its points set to a gap of ⅜in and the fence adjusted to locate them centrally. Cut the grooves to a depth of ¼in with the power router, then trim both rails to the required length and drill holes in their ends to match up exactly with the holes already marked and drilled in the legs. Drill for the dowels to match those in the under-edge of the divider.

Trim the bottom shelf to fit into its rail grooves,

cutting small notches in the corners for a neat and accurate fit.

Apply glue to all the joints, slot the bottom shelf into its housing grooves, place the metal tubing in its holes and assemble all the dowel joints. Finally, join the four legs to the top shelf assembly, and cramp up tightly until the glue has set. After removing the cramps, glasspaper the surfaces with medium and fine grade paper.

DRAWERS AND TRAY
All three drawers are designed to be opened from both sides, and there is a built-in stop preventing them from pulling right out – this simply consists of the two guide blocks fixed to the frame along which each drawer runs, see Fig. 18.8. The drawer sides are grooved to accept the blocks, but the drawer fronts act as stops to the grooves, so once they're assembled it's impossible to remove the drawers.

Cut all the drawer fronts to size, giving a clearance of ¹⁄₁₆in all round. Make the drawer sides, matching each pair of sides to the same height as the drawer fronts. Run a groove along the outside face of each side, exactly halfway down, cutting them ¾in wide and ³⁄₁₆in deep with the power router. Also, run a groove ¼in wide and ³⁄₁₆in deep along the lower inside face of each of the sides to receive the drawer bottom. A similar groove is cut on the lower inside face of each drawer front, and stopped ¼in from both ends.

The drawer fronts are assembled to the drawer sides with dowel joints; lapped dovetail joints cannot be employed here because it would be impossible to assemble the drawers properly – part of the assembly is carried out in-situ.

60

Cut the drawer bottoms from ¼in ply, matching the colour as closely as possible to the oak.

FINAL ASSEMBLY

Start by assembling and gluing up two drawer sides to one drawer front, together with the bottom. When the glue has set, fit this part-assembly into the wagon and accurately mark the position of the two grooves on to the frame. Cut the strips of wood which act as drawer guides and glue them in place halfway along the length of the end panels and the dividing panel, exactly on the line of the grooves in the sides.

Slide the half-completed drawer into position on the guide strips and fit the second drawer front. Glue on green baize to the bottom of each completed drawer with an upholstery adhesive, and fit the drawer handles – six in all.

The tray is of similar construction (Fig. 18.6), except that the sides have a tongue worked on their outside faces to slot into the grooves cut in the tray rails. Both the tray ends are given a shaped bottom edge as a decorative feature. Grooves are cut for the bottom, and the sides are dowel-jointed to the ends. Once assembled, the tray slides into its grooves and can be pulled out from either end.

Finish the whole thing off with a semi-matt polyurethane varnish, which is hard-wearing and waterproof. Fit the four castor wheels into their sockets, and you have a practical and stylish piece of mobile kitchen equipment.

CUTTING LIST

	INCHES			*MM*		
	L	W	T	L	W	T
4 legs	33⅜	1¾	1½	340	45	38
2 top side rails	19⅛	2¼	1½	485	58	38
2 top end rails	18⅜	2¼	1½	467	58	38
2 end panels	15⅛	6¼	⅝	403	159	16
1 dividing panel	18⅛	7¼	⅝	461	185	16
2 tray rails	18⅜	2	1	467	51	25
2 bottom side rails	18⅜	1¾	¾	467	45	19
2 bottom end rails	15½	1¾	¾	394	45	19
1 larger drawer front	9	6	¾	229	152	19
4 small drawer fronts	9	3⅛	¾	229	80	19
2 large drawer sides	16⅞	6	½	429	152	13
4 small drawer sides	16⅞	3⅛	¾	429	80	19
3 drawer bottoms	17¼	8⅛	¼	438	207	6
2 tray ends	15	2	¾	381	51	19
2 tray sides	18⅜	1½	⅝	467	38	16
1 tray bottom	18⅝	14¼	¼	473	362	6
1 top shelf	19	15¾	½	483	400	13
1 bottom shelf	18⅞	15⅞	½	480	403	13

Also required:– 2 lengths of brass tube 19⅛in (485mm), and 2 lengths 16⅛in (410mm); all ¾in (19mm) diameter. Working allowances have been made to lengths and widths; thicknesses are net.

SUTHERLAND GATELEG TABLE

Fig. 19.1. A sturdy and compact gateleg table.

It is often impossible to find room and a permanent position for a large table in the comparatively small rooms in modern homes, and a favoured solution to the problem is the gateleg table. This Sutherland-type table can quickly be closed and moved, as the closed size is only 36in wide by 15in deep, opening to 58in by 36in.

An attempt has been made to produce a well-designed modern piece of furniture, at the same time removing some of the faults found in this kind of table. For instance, the two lower rails are set in 6in to allow for leg room; also the battens in the flaps are finished to a thickness so that they rest against the top rails when the flaps are dawn, ensuring that the flaps hang vertically. The top of the table has been made to give maximum stability and good proportion.

The timber you choose for the top and the flaps should not show too much figure as this can detract from the uniformity of the whole design; naturally, the wood must be matched to give the best appearance and if possible all the parts should be cut from the same board.

You can use several methods for jointing the flaps, but probably the best is the rule joint fixed with three brass table leaf hinges, as it is not only efficient but neat and good looking.

FRAME CONSTRUCTION

First, prepare the wood for the underframe to length, width, and thickness. Then mark out the mortise and tenon joints for the long rails and the leg; the two top short rails can also be marked out at this juncture. Remember to leave a horn (that is, a short length of waste) on each leg at its top as this will help to prevent any splitting when cutting the mortises.

You can now cut and fit the mortises and tenons, preferably making haunched tenons to minimise any twisting that might take place in the top rail. Before marking out the two bottom short rails, you should test-fit the whole frame and check it for squareness. Mark off the rails which are set in 6in and cut and fit their mortise and tenon joints.

As the top is fixed with buttons, you can at this stage mark out the slots for them, or you can groove along the rails to save cutting the individual mortises. If you use them, there should be three mortises in each end and four on each side, and those in the end rails are made ⅛in deeper to allow for movement across the grain. The 14 buttons are made from one piece of timber, each being 1in by ¾in with a ¼in stub tenon worked on it.

GATELEG FRAMES

You can now prepare the wood for these, marking out the rails and uprights for both frames at the same time, and cutting and fitting the mortise and tenon joints.

All the edges of the six legs and rails are slightly rounded by planing, but in the case of the legs there is also a ¼in taper beginning just below the bottom rails and you will have to work this before rounding

the edges. Round the edges of the legs to approximately a ¼in radius, and the rails to a ⅛in radius; note that the bottom edges of all the legs are arrised all round about ¼in to prevent splintering during use.

The gatelegs themselves are hinged on ⅜in dia beech dowel rods, and the best method of drilling the holes for them is on a fixed vertical drill stand, but you could utilise a hand brace and bit or a portable power drill if you are careful to keep them perfectly vertical, as this is essential if you want the gatelegs to operate properly. You can drill the rails before

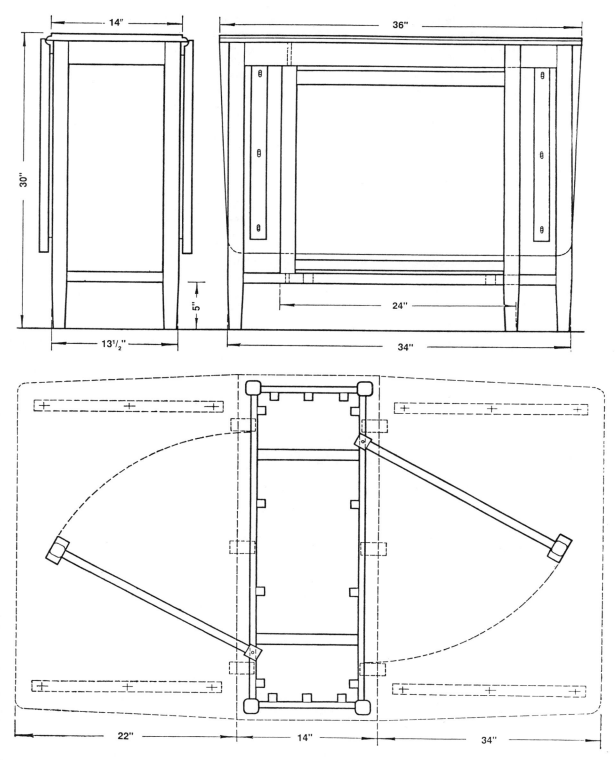

Fig. 19.2. End and side elevations; also plan.

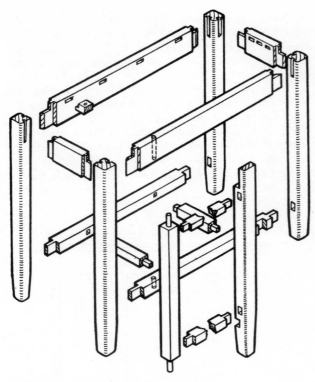

Fig. 19.3. Exploded view of construction.

gluing, but the holes in the gateleg uprights need to be drilled after gluing up the frames to give maximum accuracy.

Naturally, you will need to test-fit the gateleg frames and check them for squareness after you have cleaned them up.

THE UNDERFRAME

This is glued up in two stages with the two long frames glued first. When you have done this, test-fit the four short rails and check the assembly for squareness. If all is well, it can be glued up – if you wish, you can polish the frames before gluing up, and this is discussed later.

FITTING THE GATES

Start by removing the horns on the leg ends, then check the length of the uprights and drill the holes for the dowels; one part of the dowel is glued to the

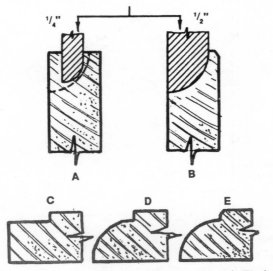

Fig. 19.4. Stages in cutting the rule joint. (A) and (B) show method of running the hollow in the leaf; (C), (D), and (E) the stages in working the round.

rail or leg in each case. The halved notches, which you will need to cut in the gateleg uprights and the underframe rails so that the gates will rest flush with the underframe when the table is closed, are best left until the fitting of the gate frames to the underframe is completed. You can mark them out more accurately at this stage although they will be more difficult to cut. The gate should rest in such a position that the three legs lie in one plane.

When you have finished working on the underframe, put on a single coat of polish to prevent the underframe becoming dirty during the rest of its time in the workshop.

THE TOP

If you are not making this from a single piece of timber, you will have to resort to rub-jointing it from several strips. You could, of course, dowel the strips together, but a rubbed joint made with a modern adhesive is extremely strong. Make sure the heart side of one strip faces in the opposite direction to that of the one alongside it, or you could eventually have a hollow table top!

Use ¾in thick timber which will finish ⅝in after planing. You must plane the edges perfectly square so that when the rule joints are cut the flaps hang in the correct plane.

THE FLAPS

The next step is to prepare these in the same manner, jointing them if necessary (three strips to each flap were used in the design shown). When you have planed the flaps flat and square, mark out and cut the 1in taper on the ends, the curve on each corner being 1in radius. The edges of the top and the flaps are taken off very slightly to a pencil edge to reduce the risk of chipping during further work.

To make sure the flaps remain flat, prepare two 1¼in by 1in battens and slot-screw them across the grain to the underside of each flap; the slot-screwing method will accommodate any slight movement that might take place in the future. Although the battens may interfere with the cutting of the rule joint, you can fix them temporarily and remove them when cutting the joint, replacing them afterwards.

WORKING THE RULE JOINT

The matching profiles of the rule joint are quite simply cut if you have the appropriate moulding planes. As this is unlikely to be the case, the job can be done either on a spindle moulder or on a power router inverted in a routing table; the latter method is probably the better as there are proprietary cutters with the exact profiles available.

Hanging the flap to the top must be done with care and should finish in end section as shown in Fig. 19.5. The hinge must be the correct table leaf type which is countersunk on the reverse side and with one leaf longer than the other. Recess the hinge leaves into the top and its flap, using three 1½in brass hinges with brass screws.

As you will need to remove the flaps several times for fitting and polishing, it is advisable to use steel screws temporarily and replace them with the brass ones on final fitting. Take care that flap does not scratch and bind when finally hinged, and it should be slightly away from the top in all positions.

The flaps must be fitted to the top while it is fixed to the underframe, as this will make it easier to plane

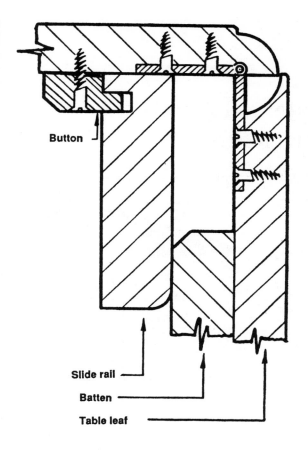

Button

Slide rail

Batten

Table leaf

Fig. 19.5. Section through rule joint hingeing – note position of the batten.

down the battens to the correct thickness so that they just rest against the top rail as shown in Fig. 19.5. Fit a stop underneath each flap in the centre and at the angle required by the gateleg frame; once fitted against this stop the gate cannot be moved without the flap being raised.

POLISHING

As already mentioned, you can do some of the polishing before gluing so that any surplus glue is easier to remove, but by using resin adhesive and removing any surplus immediately this should not be necessary. The underframe and top should be kept separate during polishing.

A plastic wood lacquer that is stain and heat resistant is the obvious choice. In between each coat, rub down with grade 00 wire wool, rubbing the last coat down lightly with the wire wool and then applying a coating of wax to give a dull sheen. Both sides of the top and flaps must be polished or there will be a risk of warping. Finally, fit the flaps and top to the underframe.

CUTTING LIST

	INCHES			MM		
	L	W	T	L	W	T
6 legs	30	1¾	1½	762	45	38
2 top long rails	34	3¼	1	863	83	25
2 top short rails	12½	3¼	¾	318	83	19
2 bottom long rails	34	1½	1¼	863	38	32
2 bottom short rails	12½	1½	1¼	318	38	32
2 gateleg top rails	23	1⅜	1	584	35	25
2 gateleg uprights	23	1½	1¼	584	38	32
2 gateleg bottom rails	23	1½	1	584	38	25
1 top bed	36½	14½	⅝	927	368	16
2 flaps	36½	22½	⅝	927	572	16
4 battens	18½	1½	1	470	38	25
2 stops	3½	2¼	½	89	58	13

Working allowances have been made to lengths and widths; thicknesses are net.

GATELEG DINING TABLE WITHOUT UNDERFRAMING

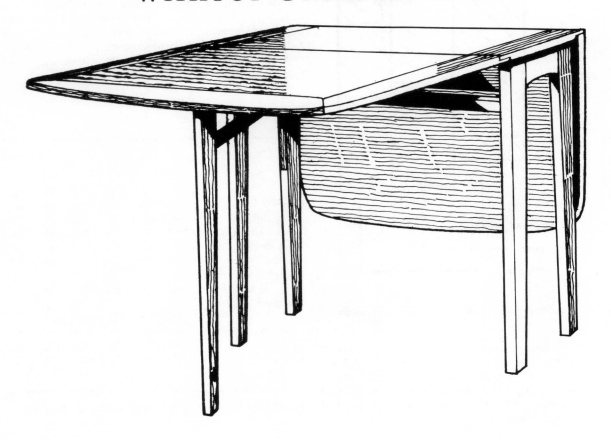

Although most hardwood timbers could be used for this contemporary dining table, teak, because of its colouring and grain, particularly enhances the appearance. The table folds to 34in by 12in by 30in high, so much space is saved and when fully open it stands 56in long by 34in wide – a useful family size.

The elimination of bottom rails, which are usual in most tables of this kind, makes for easier seating positions and does not in any way reduce the stability. You can either hinge the gateleg directly on to the side long rails with two hinges, or as a more traditional alternative, cut a knuckle hinge, which needs the variation in construction as shown in Fig. 20.5.

CONSTRUCTION

Prepare the legs and rails for the underframe to length, width and thickness, and mark out the haunched mortise and tenon joints on the corners as shown in Fig. 20.3; leave a horn at the top of each leg to prevent any chance of splitting when you are cutting the mortises. The method of allowing the tenons to meet is shown in Figs. 20.3 and 20.6.

When you have fitted the whole frame together, prepare and double-tenon a middle rail into the two long rails as in Fig. 20.6, bearing in mind that the length of this rail cannot be determined until the rest of the underframe has been put together. Make the

width of this rail ½in less than the top long rails to allow for the groove which runs around the inside of the top rails, where you can use buttons to fix the top. You can simply stub-tenon the 1¼in by ⅞in rails into the legs.

Now prepare the legs and rails for the two gates, noting that the two legs of the gates have to be ³⁄₁₆in shorter than the underframe legs so that they can fit against a stop screwed underneath the leaves of the top. You can mark out the positions of the mortises and tenons from those on the legs of the underframe. Bearing in mind that it is vital that the positions of the two rails for the gateleg are the same as the two long rails on the underframe, cut and fit these mortises and tenons.

It is a good idea to peg all mortise and tenon joints through the tenons with ¼in dia dowels while the frames lie in the cramps, as this will give added strength to the joints. Insert the dowels through from the inside to within ⅛in of the outside; glue them first into the long frames, leave the glue to set, and then clean them up before gluing the end frames. You can insert the remaining dowels into the end tenons when the whole frame has been glued. Dowel the joints on the gates when you glue them up, again working from the inside and stopping ⅛in short of the outside face; see Fig. 20.3. Next mark out and fit

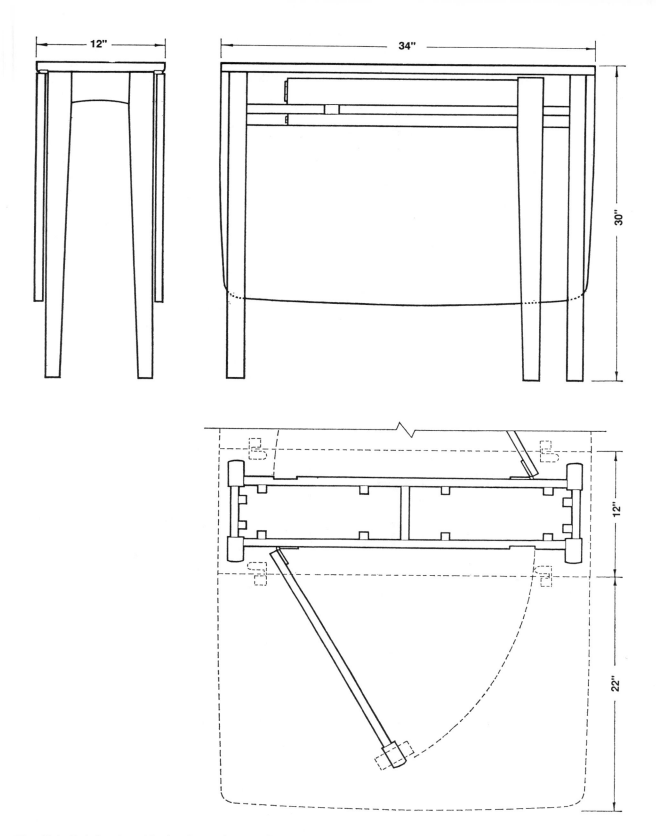

Fig. 20.1. End elevation; side elevation with nearer flap removed; plan with top shown in broken line.

the spacing pieces between the two rails on the gate, using 2in lengths of ¼in dia dowel.

You can now work the tapering of all six legs. The taper on each leg runs down to a 1½in by 1¼in rectangular section at the bottom of each leg, and each outside edge is slightly curved to the radius shown in Fig. 20.3. You can leave this part of the shaping until all the frames are glued if you do not

wish to make the appropriate cramping blocks, which, of course, would be rather difficult. Also, it is desirable that the legs should be left square at the edges to make for easier cramping as accuracy is essential, particularly when dealing with the gates. Finally, chamfer off the bottom edges of all legs to prevent damage during use and the underframe will be ready for the gluing stage.

GLUING

Clean up all inside surfaces and test-assemble the long frames of the underframe, dry. If you are satisfied that each frame is square you can glue and cramp it up, and when both are done and the glue has set you can cramp the end rails and middle rail in position, dry, to test them; if satisfactory, you can glue and cramp up the whole underframe. Remember, though, that teak is a greasy timber and the parts of the joints will need to be de-greased with something like carbon tetrachloride.

The next stage is to cramp the two gates, dry, and once the two rails are perfectly at right angles with the leg, then you can glue them. It is essential that these rails are glued at a perfect right angle otherwise they will be difficult to hinge and will certainly not swing correctly.

Cleaning up the underframe and two gates where necessary comes next, followed by the final shaping of the edges of the leg. You can also remove the horns on the legs and plane the top of the underframe flat; after glasspapering the underframe and gates you can apply one coat of teak oil.

FITTING THE GATES

The gates are fitted to the underframe by two brass hinges; on the top rail fit a 2in double leaf butt hinge, and on the thinner bottom rail a 3in strap hinge. The hinges are not recessed into the frame, as the distance between the long rail of the underframe and gate is equal to the thickness of the hinges when closed, see

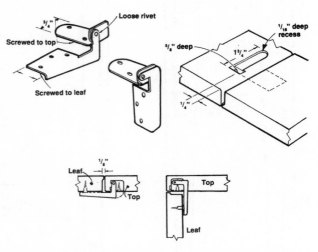

Fig. 20.2. Hingeing details. Note the shaping of the edges of the top and leaves.

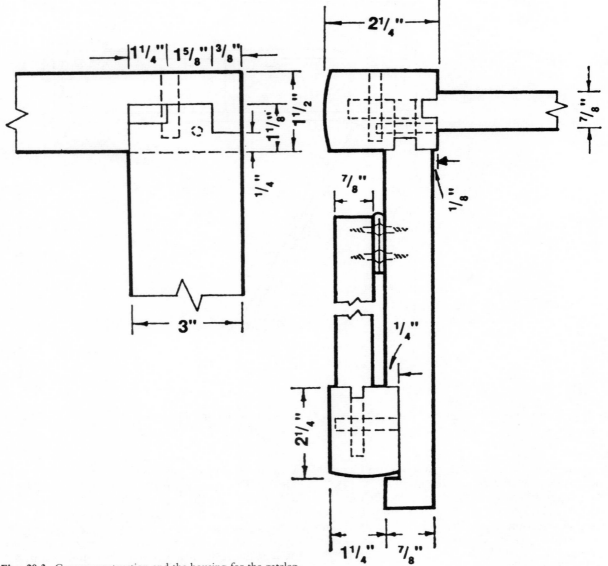

Fig. 20.3. Corner construction and the housing for the gateleg.

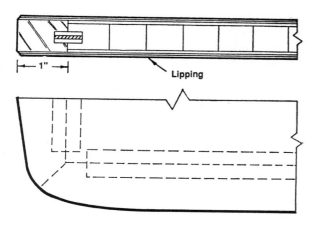

Fig. 20.4. Details of lipping.

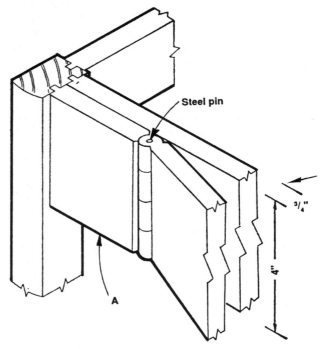

Fig. 20.5. Alternative way of hingeing the gate – the knuckle hinge.

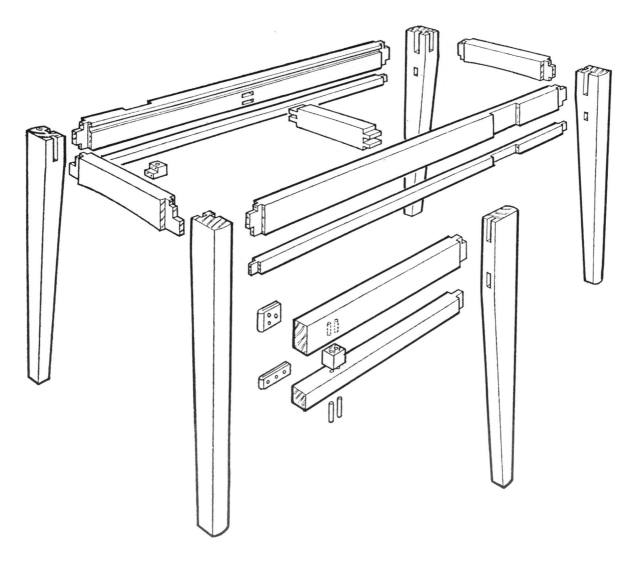

Fig. 20.6. Exploded view of construction.

Fig. 20.3. Test-fit with ¾in No 8 steel screws in the first place and when everything is working correctly, replace them with brass screws of the same size. If you use polished hinges they look very attractive when the gate is seen in its open position.

The alternative method of fixing the gates mentioned earlier means that you would need to widen the top rail of both the underframe and the gate, and use a wood knuckle joint. This would need a slightly different construction which is shown in Fig. 20.5.

When you have fixed each gate so that it opens correctly, you will have to notch a housing into the underframe rail for each gateleg so that the three legs lie flush on each side when the leaves are down; the depth of each housing is ¼in deep by 2¼in wide.

THE TOP AND LEAVES

These are made from ¾in thick blockboard, and you will need to fix a 1in wide teak lipping which is glued, using a loose tongue, around the edges with the corners mitred as in Fig. 20.4.

You will see that the sides of the top are slightly curved and it is better that the edges are shaped to this curve before veneering, as it will then be much easier to trim the veneer edges. Select the veneer carefully so that the three pieces will match when the whole of the table is open. The top is veneered on one side with teak, and you can counter-veneer the underside with gaboon, obeche, afrormosia, or sapele mahogany, depending on the amount you want to spend! It is worth rounding off the edges to a pencil finish to reduce the likelihood of damage to the veneer during use and the easiest way is to use a glasspaper block and a light hand.

The hingeing edges require slight shaping as shown in Fig. 20.2. You can shoot the edges of the bed quite simply with a jack plane, but you will need a rebate plane for the edge of each leaf.

You can see the fixing of the special brass table-leaf hinges from Fig. 20.2; two are required for each leaf. Screw each one on in the position shown and finally fit it into the mortise which has been cut to accept it in the top. When hanging, the leaves fall beneath the top but when open butt against the edge of the top.

FINAL JOBS

You can fit the leaves before the underframe is fixed on to the top; this fixing is effected by means of twelve buttons which are screwed to the underside of the top and fit into the inside edge of the underframe, as already mentioned.

An alternative method is to use brass strips screwed on to the top rails and you can then screw through them into the top.

When the final fitting of hinges and buttons has been done, remove them and give the top a final rub down with 00 glasspaper and apply one coat of teak oil. Then rub down both the top and the underframe once more with 00 glasspaper and apply more coats of teak oil as advised by the manufacturer; you can then re-hinge and refit the top and the leaves.

CUTTING LIST

	INCHES			MM		
	L	W	T	L	W	T
1 top bed	33	11½	¾	838	292	19
2 flaps, each	33	20½	¾	838	521	19
6 legs	30	2½	1½	762	64	38
2 long frieze rails	32	3¼	⅞	813	83	22
3 short frieze rails	11	3¼	⅞	279	83	22
2 long rails	32	1¼	⅞	813	32	22
2 short rails	24	3	⅞	609	76	22
2 rails	24	1¼	⅞	609	32	22
Lippings						
6 pieces	36	1¼	1	915	32	25
4 pieces	24	1¼	1	609	32	25
2 pieces	13	1¼	1	330	32	25

Working allowances have been made to lengths and widths; thicknesses are net.

TEAK SIDEBOARD WITH PART-TAMBOUR FRONT

This sideboard, which was made in teak, affords an opportunity to make a really modern piece of furniture in the traditional manner, yet having experimental features such as the pre-formed drawer handles. The general concept of the design is described below and, if followed closely, you should be able to exploit fully all its subtleties.

GENERAL DESCRIPTION
Choose a straightgrained veneer for the carcase and avoid a decorative pattern – to harmonise with this, choose a figured veneer for the drawer fronts. The tambour front helps to relieve the monotony of the flat areas and accentuate the sideboard front.

The underframing plays an important part in the appearance: in particular, note how the axis of each leg follows through the centre line of the handles, and also that the length of the underframing is equal to the inside dimensions of the carcase; these two factors help to bond the two separate elements together.

The sliding action of the tambour is concealed by a false end and back, and these also prevent articles inside the cabinet obstructing the action of the tambour.

PREPARATION AND CONSTRUCTION
In view of the size of the sideboard and the need for the tambour action to work smoothly, you will find it best to make all the panels in laminated board, veneered on both sides and with the edges lipped where necessary. By doing this you will eliminate the twin bugbears of shrinkage and distortion. Laminated board ¾in thick with a ⅜in wide core was used for the carcase, the false ends and intermediate partitions being in plywood.

Start by cutting panels from the laminated board to width, taking into account the additional widths

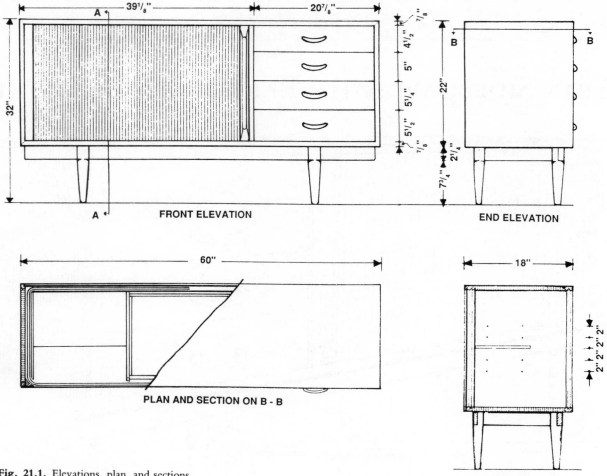

Fig. 21.1. Elevations, plan, and sections.

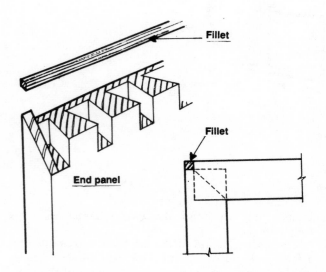

Fig. 21.2. Diagrammatic view of end panel, with section showing fillet.

of the lippings. Square off the ends of the panels, and deduct ³⁄₁₆in from their length to allow for the double lap-dovetails where they are used.

When you have glued the lippings in position, they should project ³⁄₁₆in at each end to allow you to work a mitre on the front and back of the corner joint.

After you have veneered the panels, trim the veneer round the lippings and ends. By cutting the panels ³⁄₁₆in short of the length and making the lippings the full length, you will avoid the extra work of rebating to take the fillet. It is not necessary

to deduct ³⁄₁₆in in the length for the bottom carcase joints, which are straightforward orthodox lap-dovetails. Make sure that the lippings are the full thickness and then plane to the correct thickness when in position.

Prepare the panels for veneering in the normal manner. Their surfaces must be perfectly flat and toothed to provide an adequate key for the glue. When using teak, either in veneer form or in the solid, it is always best to remove the natural grease from the surface before gluing, and you can do this by wiping it over with methylated spirits or a proprietary de-greasing liquid. After veneering, plane the panels to the correct width, square the ends, and cut them to the appropriate length.

The joints for the carcase are as follows: double lap-dovetails for the top two joints, lap-dovetails at the bottom corners, and all intermediate panels housed in at both the top and bottom. The double lap-dovetail differs slightly from the conventional joint in that a ³⁄₁₆in square fillet is substituted for the lap, as you can see from Fig. 21.2. Fix this fillet in position after the carcase has been assembled, and it will ensure that no end grain veneer is left to show. Consequently, all the other veneered edges have a ¹⁄₁₆in rebate taken out, the purpose of this being two-fold; first, to prevent damage to the edge of the veneer; and second, to reduce the thickness of the panels.

You will find it advisable to cut the required grooves for the tambour, the false back, and the back proper, before finally assembling the carcase. In the

72

Fig. 21.3. Exploded view of construction (carcase joints omitted for clarity)

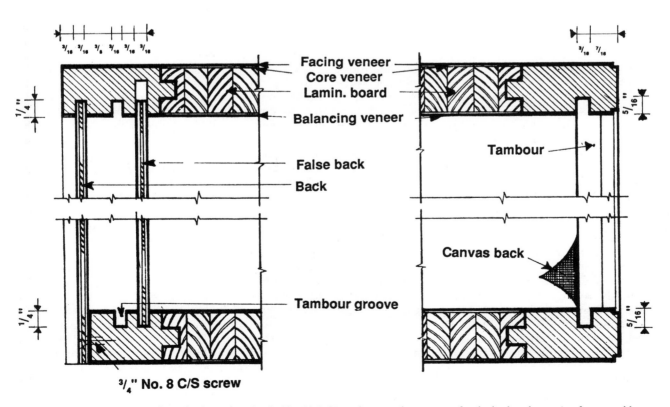

Fig. 21.4. Part section A–A from the front elevation in Fig. 21.1. Note the extra deep groove for the back to be put in after assembly; also, the rebate at the front edges to protect the edges of the veneer.

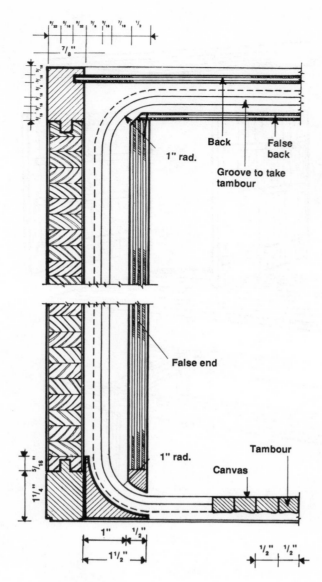

Fig. 21.5. Section through B–B.

Fig. 21.6. Leg and rail assembly.

section A–A, Fig. 21.4, you will see that the groove to take the false back is deeper at the top than at the bottom and this is to allow you to place the back in position after assembly.

For convenience it is best to omit all interior panels and backs until the fitting and running of the tambour is completed, and this also applies to the corner block that conceals the tambour when it is closed.

THE UNDERFRAMING

This is quite straightforward in construction and is illustrated in Figs. 21.1, 21.3, and 21.6. As you can see from Fig. 21.6, the cross rails are dowelled into the legs, the dowels securing the long rails to the legs.

When you turn the legs, be sure to finish them slightly convex. If you give them a straight taper they will appear hollow and lacking in strength when the underframe is assembled. The timber for the whole of the underframe should be as near in character (colour, texture, etc) to that of the carcase veneer.

DRAWERS AND TRAYS

These are made in the conventional manner, as shown in Figs. 21.7 and 21.8; the sides of both are grooved to take the runners. You have a choice of

methods for fixing the runners to the carcase interior, you can groove them into the panels (which should be done before assembling the carcase), or you can simply glue and screw them on and this is quite strong enough for the purpose.

In our design, the drawers and trays were made in mahogany, with the drawers having teak veneered fronts.

THE TAMBOUR

Before making this it is well worthwhile making a jig in which to hold the pieces collectively for gluing on the canvas backing, and later for shouldering the ends; the jig is shown in Fig. 21.9.

You can plot the profile of the tambour sections from Fig. 21.5, and as you can see, they are slightly hollow on the face and have rounded edges. If you have a spindle moulder or a router which you can invert in a router-table, either of them will ease the work considerably; if not, you will have to work the individual pieces with a moulding plane and/or scratch stock. Use a suitably profiled block when glasspapering them.

Cut the tambour pieces roughly to length and then feed them into the jig, face down, so that you can glue the canvas to their backs; you may have to cramp down a spare piece of board over them to apply the necessary pressure.

Once the canvas is firmly stuck down, remove one side of the jig and introduce a packing piece at the other side so that one edge of the tambour projects over the side of the jig. This will allow you to cramp it in the jig, cut it to width, square it off straight, and cut the shoulders. The tenons on the ends of each tambour strip are ⅜in by 3⁄16in and of appropriate length to fit the groove in which they run.

Allow an overhang of canvas at one end of the completed set of tambours to which you can fasten the thicker handle piece. The hollow of the handle is ¾in by ⅜in deep and rounded at the ends, the handle

74

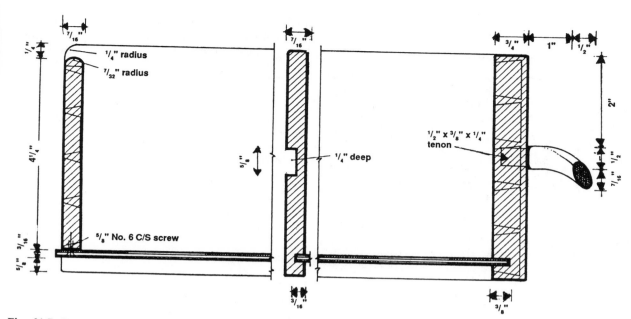

Fig. 21.7. Section through one of the drawers.

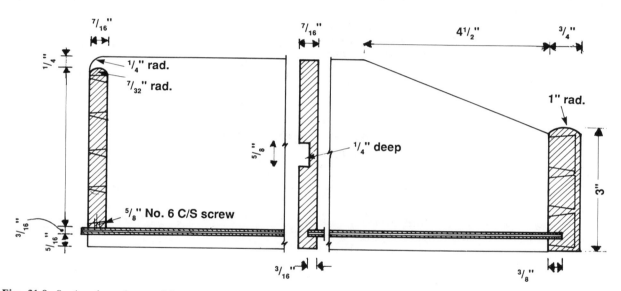

Fig. 21.8. Section through one of the trays.

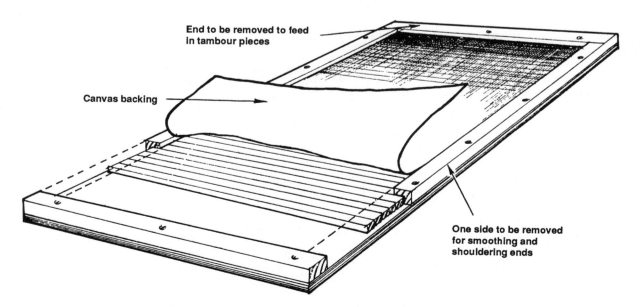

Fig. 21.9. Jig for making the tambours. When one side of the jig is removed for shooting and shouldering, a packing piece is put in the other side so that the tambour overlaps one side.

75

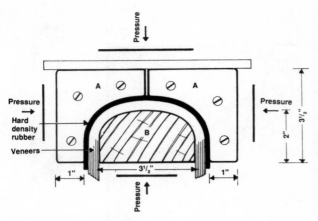

Fig. 21.10. Suggested method for making the handles. (A) is the female mould, (B) is the male. The arrows indicate the direction of cramping pressure. Cramping must be arranged progressively so that excess glue is squeezed out.

piece being reduced in thickness at the top and bottom and having its shoulders cut in a similar way to the other tambours.

To fix the handle, the canvas should be taken round a batten and glued and screwed through to the back of the handle piece. This will, among other things, stop any slight excess of glue which might squeeze through from sticking between the separate pieces.

Feed the tambour into its groove from the back of the carcase, and you will have to cut a special short groove for the purpose which is filled when the tambour is in place. You can apply a light coat of wax to the tenons and shoulders to help them to run smoothly.

HANDLES

Those for the drawers are pre-formed from teak veneers, and the most suitable hand method is to employ male and female formers. You can make the female former from offcuts of blockboard, shaped roughly, screwed together, and finally shaped; the male former can be made from softwood.

Although you can make the formers big enough to turn out all four handles at one time, you will probably find it easier to make them in pairs. Insert a piece of high density rubber sheeting between the female formers and the veneers to absorb any slight irregularities in the mould. From Fig. 21.10 you can see that the female mould is made in two parts so that you can apply adequate pressure in the correct places. As the bend of the veneers is fairly acute, they can be soaked, bent to shape, and allowed to dry before you apply the glue for the actual fabrication; you can, of course, use any suitable cramps to apply the pressure.

After you have taken the 'form' from the mould you can carry out the final shaping with care. Make a cardboard template so all the handles turn out exactly the same shape, and the section shown in Fig. 21.7 should be followed closely. Cut the tenons on the handle ends next and finally glue the handles into mortises cut for them in the drawer fronts.

FINISH

After you have cleaned up and glasspapered all the parts in the normal way, apply one coat of white polish to seal the grain, and glasspaper it lightly; then apply the teak oil in accordance with the manufacturer's instructions. One last point – you will find it best to polish all interior parts before assembly.

CUTTING LIST

	INCHES			MM		
Carcase	L	W	T	L	W	T
1 top	60½	14½	¾	1536	368	19
1 bottom	60½	14½	¾	1536	368	19
2 ends, each	22½	14½	¾	571	368	19
2 partitions, each	21¾	16½	¾	553	419	19
1 false end, ply	21¾	15¾	½	553	401	13
1 false back, ply	40	21½	³/₁₆	1016	546	5
1 back	60	22	³/₁₆	1524	559	5
Lippings						
3 lippings, each	60½	2	⅞	1536	51	22
1 lipping	60½	1¾	⅞	1536	45	22
6 lippings, each	22½	2	⅞	571	51	22
1 lipping	22½	1¼	⅝	571	32	16
1 lipping	16¼	¾	⅝	413	19	16
2 fillets	18¼	⁵/₁₆	³/₁₆	464	8	5
Underframe						
2 rails	60	2½	1	1524	64	25
2 rails	12½	2½	1	318	64	25
4 legs	11	2¼	2	279	58	51
Trays & drawers						
3 tray bottoms, ply	18	16	³/₁₆	457	406	5
4 drawer bottoms, ply	20	17	³/₁₆	508	432	5
1 tray front	18½	3¼	¾	470	83	19
1 tray front	18½	3¾	¾	470	95	19
1 tray front	18½	4¼	¾	470	108	19
2 tray sides	15½	4¾	⁷/₁₆	394	121	11
2 tray sides	15½	5½	⁷/₁₆	394	140	11
2 tray sides	15½	6¼	⁷/₁₆	394	159	11
1 tray back	18½	4¼	⁷/₁₆	470	108	11
1 tray back	18½	4¾	⁷/₁₆	470	121	11
1 tray back	18½	5¾	⁷/₁₆	470	146	11
1 drawer front	20½	4¾	¾	521	121	19
1 drawer front	20½	5¼	¾	521	134	19
1 drawer front	20½	5½	¾	521	140	19
1 drawer front	20½	5¾	¾	521	146	19
2 drawer sides	17	4¾	⁷/₁₆	432	121	11
2 drawer sides	17	5¼	⁷/₁₆	432	134	11
2 drawer sides	17	5½	⁷/₁₆	432	140	11
2 drawer sides	17	5¾	⁷/₁₆	432	146	11
1 drawer back	20½	4	⁷/₁₆	521	102	11
1 drawer back	20½	4½	⁷/₁₆	521	115	11
1 drawer back	20½	4¾	⁷/₁₆	521	121	11
1 drawer back	20½	5	⁷/₁₆	521	127	11
14 drawer runners	16½	¾	⅜	419	19	10
Tambours						
90 tambour strips, each	22	⅝	½	559	16	13
1 tambour handle	22	2	¾	559	51	19
Miscellaneous						
1 corner piece	22	1¾	1¾	559	45	45
1 shelf, ply	16½	9½	⅝	419	241	16

Veneers for drawer handles

Working allowances have been made to lengths and widths; thicknesses are net.

A 'Running Sideboard' or Dinner Wagon

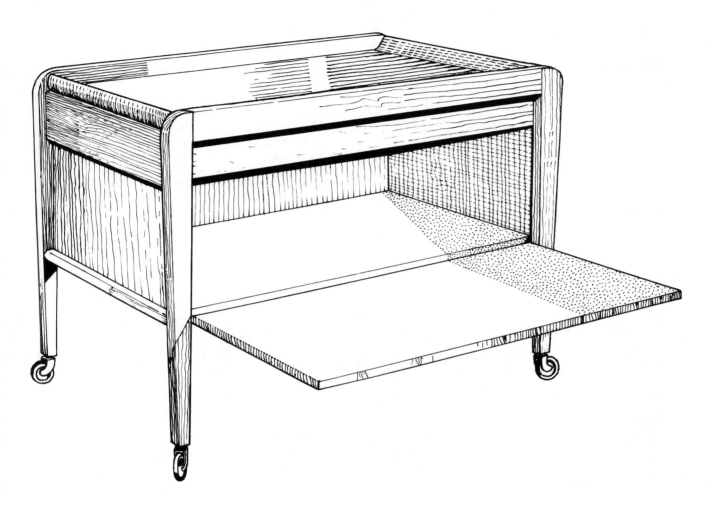

In 18th century America, this kind of design was known as a 'running sideboard' and the name was also later used in Britain although it has now been supplanted by the term 'dinner wagon' – both refer to a piece of furniture that carries food and crockery and can be wheeled into and around a dining room.

The design should have the inside surfaces of the fall sides and the bottom faced with a plastic laminate, and one of the drawers should be baize-lined for cutlery. It could be divided into sections (but this is not allowed for in the cutting list), while the other drawer could be polished inside to hold napkins and the like.

SIDES
After you have cut the timber into rough sizes, prepare the sub-assemblies, each consisting of two legs and a top rail. Note that the legs taper from 2½in at the top to 1¼in at the bottom, and the top outer corner of each leg is roughly rounded to a 2½in radius as shown in Figs. 22.1 and 22.2

Temporarily cramp the legs together and mark across all four at the same time so that you obtain uniformity in height for setting out the panel grooves; at the same time you can mark the positions of the dowel holes to take the top, middle, and bottom end rails, and the top side rails.

You can now cut the top side rails to length, and groove them on their inside faces to accept the top tongues and the ends dowelled into the legs. Check that the ends are square before gluing together.

TOP
Veneer the panel for this on both sides. The veneer used will depend on the finish required, but should be laid in the direction shown in the plan in Fig. 22.2, that is, at right angles to the sides. When the glue has set, cut to size and square up the top.

Next, groove the sides and ends to receive the tongues as indicated in Figs. 22.1 and 22.2, and prepare the moulded end pieces – mark the curves required for these with a template.

Square up the edges to be joined to the panel and slot them to receive the tongues; all the slots are

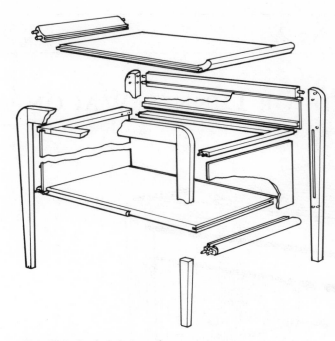

Fig. 22.1. Exploded view of construction.

uniform in width and depth and are ¼in by ⁷⁄₁₆in respectively. The inside curve is best worked with a moulding plane if you have one but you could use a gouge instead.

It is as well to leave the shaping of the outer curve until the various sub-assemblies have been glued and cramped together as this will lessen the likelihood of damage. Bore the ends for dowels and glue and cramp the parts together.

BOTTOM

Build this up in a similar manner to the top. It consists of a blockboard sheet with end pieces grooved to take a plywood panel which is tongued on.

Cut a piece of plastic laminate to size and fix it to the upper surface, arranging the ends to be in line with each inside edge of the panel grooves so that when these are placed in position they butt against the inside face. Pin and glue a lipping strip equal in width to the thickness of the blockboard plus the plastic laminate to the sides to cover edge. When you have prepared this lipping, bore dowel holes through it into the end pieces for jointing to the legs.

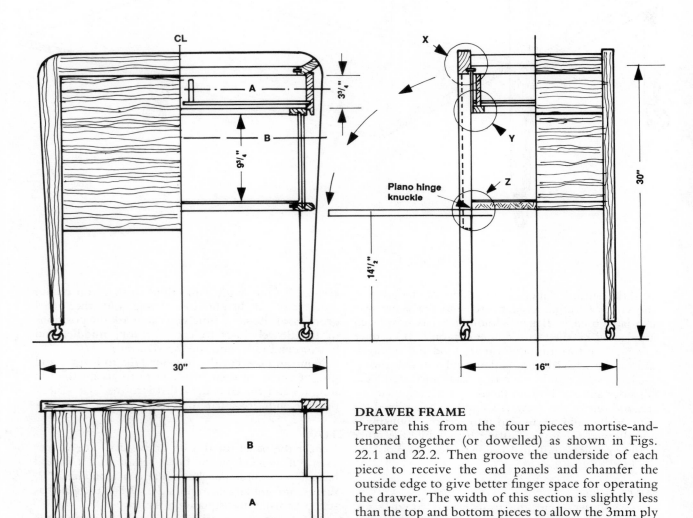

Fig. 22.2. Elevations, plan, and sections. Enlarged details of (X), (Y), and (Z) are given in Fig. 22.3.

DRAWER FRAME

Prepare this from the four pieces mortise-and-tenoned together (or dowelled) as shown in Figs. 22.1 and 22.2. Then groove the underside of each piece to receive the end panels and chamfer the outside edge to give better finger space for operating the drawer. The width of this section is slightly less than the top and bottom pieces to allow the 3mm ply panels (Fig. 22.2) to come between it and the legs.

PANELS

Veneer the side panels on both faces before cutting to size; lay the veneer with the grain running as indicated in Fig. 22.2.

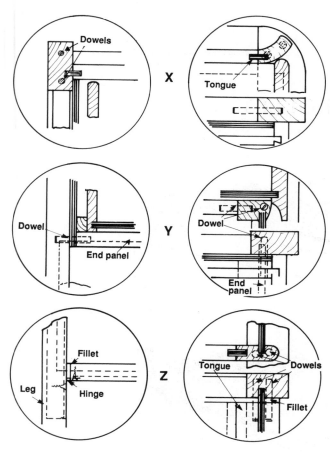

Fig. 22.3. Enlarged details of (X), (Y), and (Z) from Fig 22.2.

ASSEMBLY

Now, glue and pin the narrow side panels in position on the rail and leg units. Lay one of the leg assemblies on its side, and locate and glue in the top, the middle frame, the bottom, and the end panels, all in one operation. You can now fit the remaining leg assembly and cramp the whole thing together, testing for squareness before the adhesive finally sets.

DRAWERS

These are made up in the traditional way, the bottom being fitted into the front and sides, and screwed or pinned to the underside of the back. As the front overlaps the sides, you will find it advisable to lap-dovetail them into the front. Both fronts are moulded at the top and bottom as in Fig 22.2, the sides, backs, and bottoms being worked accordingly. Note that a guide, (Y) in Fig. 22.2, is glued to the drawer frame to give extra rigidity to the side panels. Arrange both fronts to stand proud at the end; the narrow plywood panel and drawer guide ends should act as stops.

FLAPS

You should veneer the exterior faces of these before cutting them to size; a sheet of plastic laminate is stuck to the inner surface of each flap to butt against the hinge knuckle.

For a professional-looking finish, you can veneer the edges with crossgrained veneer. You could, alternatively, lip them in which case you will need to stick down the plastic laminate first, followed by the lipping, finishing off by laying the surface veneer.

You can fix lengths of piano (continuous) hinge to fasten the falls to the bottom as shown in Fig. 22.2; after the hinge has been fixed, an extra strip of plastic sheeting is glued on extending from the end of the hinge flap to the bottom edge of the falls for levelling purposes.

Other fittings comprise quadrant stays which could be fixed to the falls if you wish, and ball catches to hold the flaps when closed; four good quality sprung trolley castors are also needed.

CUTTING LIST

	INCHES			MM		
	L	W	T	L	W	T
Main frame						
4 legs	30½	2⅞	1¼	775	73	32
2 side rails	25½	3	1¼	648	76	32
1 top★	14½	25½	¾	369	648	19
2 top end pieces	14½	3	1½	369	76	38
1 bottom★	14½	25½	¾	369	648	19
2 bottom end pieces	14½	3	⅞	369	76	22
Drawer frame						
2 rails	24	1¾	¾	609	45	19
2 rails	14	2½	1	356	64	25
2 side panels★	27	5	⅛	686	127	3
2 end panels★	15½	11	¼	394	279	6
Drawers						
2 fronts	15	5½	⅞	381	140	22
4 sides	13	4	⅝	330	102	16
2 backs	13	3¾	⅝	330	95	16
2 bottoms	13	13½	3/16	330	343	4
2 guides	27	1	½	686	25	13
Falls						
2 pieces★	25½	17½	¾	648	445	19
1 piece plastic laminate	26	14½		660	369	
2 pieces plastic laminate	25½	18		648	458	

Note:— in items marked ★, the longest dimension indicates the grain direction if veneer is used.

Working allowances have been made to lengths and widths; thicknesses are net.

TEA TROLLEY

Not only is this trolley attractive in appearance, but the trays are designed for easy cleaning. The drawer is an inconspicuous feature that will hold tea knives, spoons, napkins etc, and a hand grip cut into the bottom edge of the drawer front makes it less obvious as a drawer when closed.

If you haven't the facilities for making them you may feel that the laminated trays render the trolley too difficult to make, but there is no reason why you should not substitute flat trays for the laminated ones, and Fig. 23.5 shows an alternative design which gives effect to this.

The bases are of 6mm plywood faced with a plastic laminate on the working surfaces, and you will need to cut away the corners to fit round the trolley legs. Then you can screw the four rebated mouldings as shown along the straight edges of the trays to complete them.

VACUUM BAG PRESS
This is necessary to make up the laminated trays and you will not find it too difficult to improvise one. In principle the process consists of placing the work (in this case, the laminations plus a former) inside a bag and then evacuating the air to create a vacuum which will pull the laminations into the desired shape around the former.

No doubt you will immediately think of using a domestic vacuum cleaner to evacuate the air and this will do the job well enough. In addition you will need a strong, flexible, and airtight bag, and a stout gauge plastic one should be suitable. Once the work is inside the bag, seal the open end except for one corner where you insert the nozzle of the cleaner; use strong adhesive tape of the kind sold for making up parcels for this.

Such a set-up should enable you to do this particular job, but if you want a vacuum bag press as a piece of workshop equipment then you will need a vacuum pump instead of the cleaner, and a bag made of some really robust material such as Neoprene.

LAMINATING
First, make up a former by gluing together two pieces of ¾in thick blockboard as shown in Fig. 23.5, and round the edges to a radius of 1½in.

Next, roughly shape the corners of the pieces of plywood for the laminates, leaving a little for trimming up after they are glued together, and alternating

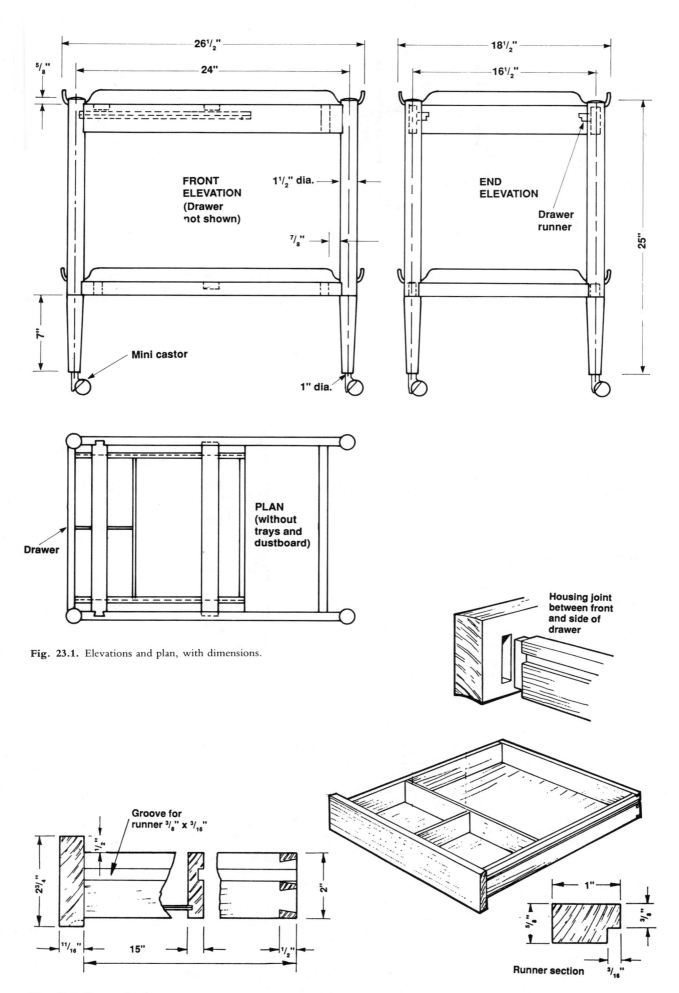

Fig. 23.1. Elevations and plan, with dimensions.

Fig. 23.2. Drawer details.

81

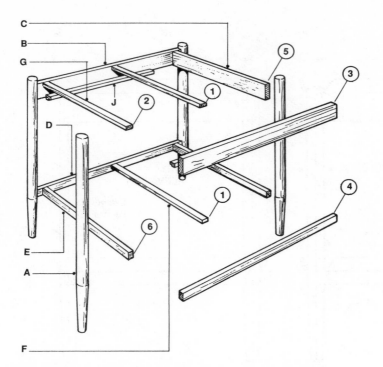

Fig. 23.3. Exploded view of construction showing joints used.

the grain direction of each piece. Make a paper or card template to fit in the trolley frame so that you are sure of a correct size for the blanks.

The next step is to soak the sheets of ply for some hours in lukewarm water to make them pliable. Then put four sheets, without glue, on the former in the vacuum press and evacuate the air, leaving the set-up overnight. When you remove the blanks they will retain their shapes quite well.

APPLYING THE PLASTIC FACING
Before you finally glue the sheets together, obtain a sheet of the thinnest plastic laminate you can, so that it is flexible enough for you to bend it to shape after cutting away the corners.

The bending is best done by gently warming the back of the material over a gas flame and putting it on to the former quickly and into the vacuum bag before it has time to cool. Leave it for some time after evacuating the air for it to retain the desired shape. Experiment with some practice runs, using scrap material, to judge how best to achieve the required flexibility.

Finally, you can press and stick the plywood and plastic laminate together in one operation using a contact adhesive – be sure to place newspaper or a piece of plastic film between the former and the blanks to stop them adhering to each other.

When the adhesive has set, all that remains to be done is to trim and round off the edges, fit the trays into the trolley frame and give the wood surfaces a coat of polyester lacquer.

OPTIONAL DUSTBOARD
You may like to leave the top tray loose so that it can be used separately; if so, it would be advisable to insert a dustboard in the frame to cover the drawer when you remove the tray.

This does not involve much change in the making up of the trolley frame. The top side rails, the end rail, and the end support rail have to be rebated and the central cross support rail reduced in thickness to

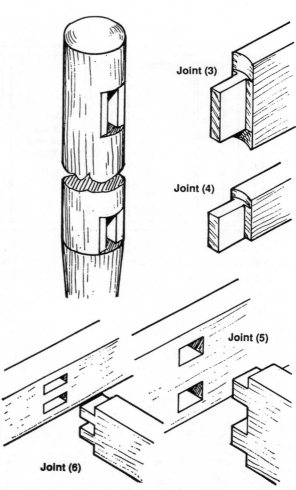

Fig.23.4. The various joints – the numbers refer to Fig. 23.3.

accommodate the dustboard, which is made of 4mm plywood. It is not shown in the illustrations as it is optional.

THE TROLLEY FRAME
Make up the two side frames first. The legs have to be turned, but it is better to cut the mortises in them,

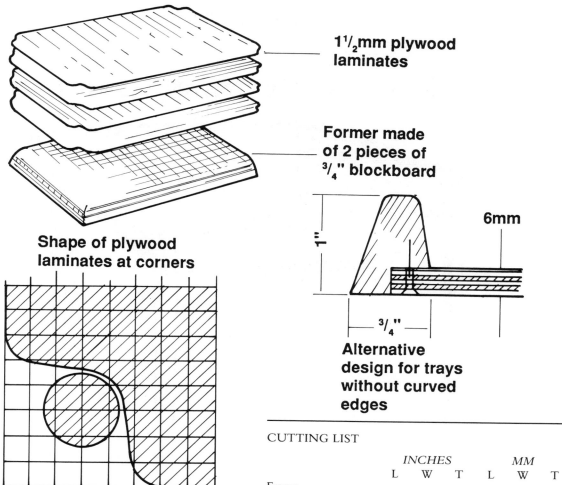

1¹⁄₂mm plywood laminates

Shape of plywood laminates at corners

Former made of 2 pieces of ³⁄₄" blockboard

6mm

1"

³⁄₄"

Alternative design for trays without curved edges

¹⁄₂" squares

Fig. 23.5. Tray details and alternative designs.

(Figs 23.3 and 23.4) while the legs are still in the square. Of course, you will have to plug the mortises with scrap wood for the turning to be done. Notice that the ends of the tenon shoulders are scribed to fit the curvature of the legs except for the length of each mortise where the leg surfaces are flatted off.

Have a trial assembly of the side frames while marking out the joints on the cross rails; you can then cut and fit them. The two stages in the final assembly are to glue up the side frames first, and then to glue in all the cross rails to square up the frame.

THE DRAWER
From the plan, Fig. 23.1, and also from Fig. 23.2 you will see that the ends of the drawer front are scribed over the legs so that the drawer occupies the same relative position as the side rails. This makes it necessary to use a tongued housing joint where each side is attached to the front, and each joint needs to be made a tight fit to resist the pulling strain when the drawer is opened.

The rest of the drawer construction is orthodox; the bottom is grooved into the front, the back and the sides, and the partitions are fixed in housing joints. Note that the drawer sides have to be suitably grooved for sliding on the runners; the latter are screwed accurately in position on the inside faces of the side rails and the drawer fitted by easing them with a block plane or a bullnose plane.

CUTTING LIST

	INCHES			MM		
	L	W	T	L	W	T
Frame						
Part						
A 4 legs	25½	1¾	1½	648	45	38
B 2 top side rails	25	2¾	¾	635	70	19
C 1 top end rail	17	2¾	¾	432	70	19
D 2 bottom side rails	25	1½	¾	635	38	19
E 2 bottom end rails	17	1½	¾	432	38	19
F 1 bottom support rail	16½	1½	⅝	419	38	16
G 2 top support rails	16½	1½	½	419	38	13
2 drawer runners	15	1¼	⅝	381	32	16
Laminated trays						
8 pieces of plywood	29½	21¼	¹⁄₁₆	749	540	1.5
2 pieces of plastic laminate	29½	21¼	–	749	540	–
Flat trays						
2 pieces of plywood	24½	16¼	¼	622	413	6
2 pieces of plastic laminate	24½	16¼	–	622	413	–
4 mouldings	23	1¼	¾	584	32	19
4 mouldings	15	1¼	¾	381	32	19
Drawer						
1 front	16	3	¹¹⁄₁₆	406	76	18
2 sides	16	2¼	½	406	58	13
1 back	13⅛	2¼	½	333	58	13
1 cross-partition	12⅝	1⅞	¼	321	48	6
1 partition	6	1⅞	¼	152	48	6
1 base	15¼	12¼	³⁄₁₆	388	311	4

Working allowances have been made to lengths and widths; thicknesses are net.

Loose-leaf Extending Table

Fig. 24.1. A small dining table with a big top – it is in two parts that pull out, enabling a separate loose leaf to be fitted.

The closed size of this table, 45in by 36in, and opening to just over 57in by 36in is convenient for the average dining room, but if necessary you could reduce the width to 33in. There are two sliding tops which pull out to enable a loose leaf to be dropped in; these tops have slides fixed to their undersides which engage with bearers screwed to the side rails. Stops regulate the closed position of the tops, and wood springs fitted beneath prevent them from being pulled right out. By depressing the springs, however, it is always possible to withdraw the tops entirely if required.

The tops are made from ¾in gaboon multi-ply veneered in a parquet design – it might be possible to obtain plywood parquet blocks, but the size of the table would have to be altered to suit the standard sizes of the blocks.

An oak lipping is tongued in and mitred round; if you prefer, you could veneer both sides with plain veneer, adding the lipping afterwards. Other alternatives for the top are laminboard or good grade chipboard.

FRAMEWORK

This consists of ⅞in rails tenoned into turned legs which finish 2¼in at the top. There are no squares on the legs, the rails being taken directly into the round, and the simplest way of arranging the joint is to cut flats on the legs opposite the joints as in Fig. 24.6. If you have a mortiser you can do this accurately by fitting a rotary miller bit which will enable the flats to be cut at right angles, and the mortises with their haunches can afterwards be made with the same tool. You could arrange for rather longer tenons by offsetting the mortises towards the outside. This kind of bit makes a mortise with rounded ends and you will need to chop them out square. If you have to work entirely by hand you will have to set out the flats accurately as shown in Fig. 24.5. Prepare a special V–shaped block to hold the rounded leg, its width being the same diameter as the leg. One diagonal at the end can be marked by squaring up from the bottom. Use a mortise gauge to mark the lines of the flats and the mortise lines; you will have to cramp the block to the leg while doing so.

Cutting the flats by hand means using a chisel and finishing off with a file; or you could alternatively make up a jig so that you could use a shoulder plane on its top edges. Another way would be to mark and chop out the mortises while the wood is still square; the mortises can then be plugged temporarily and the legs turned. But if you do this, exact centering is essential.

Put the two ends of the table together independently and allow the glue to set before adding the

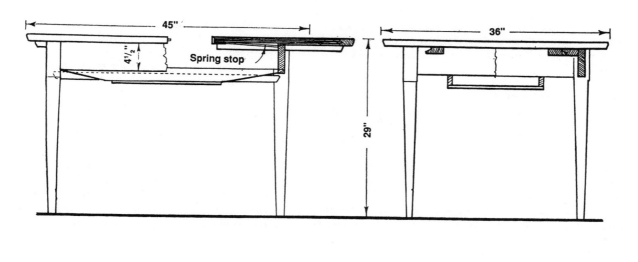

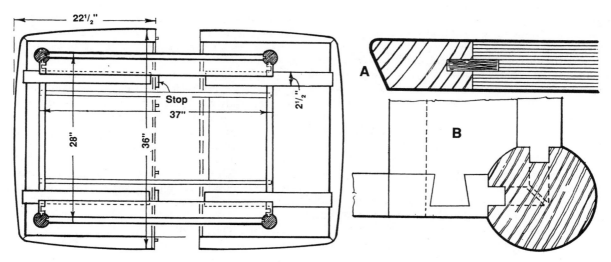

Fig. 24.2. Elevations and plan. Also, at (A), detail of the top edge lipping; at (B), jointing the leg into corner of frame.

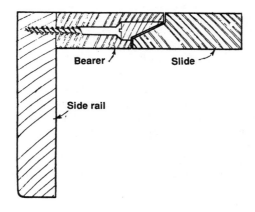

Fig. 24.3. Section through a rail showing slides and bearers.

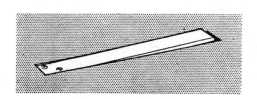

Fig. 24.4. Sketch of the spring stop.

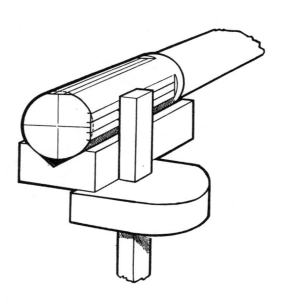

Fig. 24.5. Marking the flats and mortises on a leg.

remaining rail; note that the lower outer edges of the rails are radiused as in Fig. 24.3 to give a neat finish and to prevent injuring your knees when you are sitting at the table.

BEARERS AND SLIDES

Rebated bearers are fixed to the framework sides, and corresponding slides beneath the tops. Often square rebates are cut halfway in both, but it makes a stronger job if they are sloped as in Fig. 24.3. The root of the rebate is the part most subjected to strain, and the slope means that both are wider at this point.

Use lapped dovetails to fix the bearers to the end rails, and remember to position the dovetails so that they clear the rebates (see Fig. 24.6). Counter-bore for the screws used along the length, and be sure to bore the holes before the rebates are worked (see Fig. 24.3). To work the rebates, plane down as far as the highest part, using a fillister or rebate plane, and finish at the angle down as far as a line gauged at the edge.

Insert the dovetails, dry, and mark inside the line of the sloping rebate. Square down a line giving the width of the slide, and mark in the thickness with a gauge. Remove the waste by sawing across the grain and chopping it away with a chisel. Clearly, the sloping cut must align with that of the bearer, and when nearly down to the line put in the bearer, gluing right along the edge and screwing it in position. You can level off any unevenness at the notch afterwards.

Since the slides are of the same section as the bearers you can prepare them at the same time. Each is fitted individually into its notch and numbered to enable it to be replaced in the same position. Bore and countersink the screw holes for fixing.

VENEERING THE PARQUET TOPS

Prepare the parquet pattern for the tops by cutting the veneer into strips, and trim them to exactly 2in

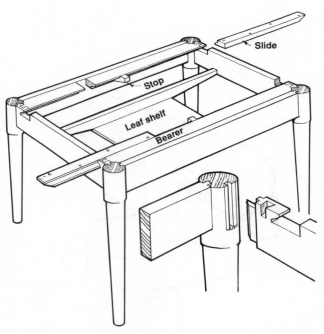

Fig. 24.6. View with the tops removed to show how the slides fit in the bearers. Note the stops which ensure that the tops are centred; the ends of the slides butt against them. The slides should be about ⅝in short of the inner top edges.

wide. As the squares are 8in long it follows that some strips have to be 8in long, while others are 4in. You will probably find it convenient to prepare the veneers in packs and use a jig for trimming them to size. The same thing applies to length trimming, which is best done on a shooting board fitted with a length stop. Thus, one end can be trimmed first held against the stop while the other is prepared. You'll need 56 strips 8in long, and 96 of 4in, but it's worth cutting some extra.

To assemble the main squares, fit an edging at the corner of a square board and place the veneers in position as at (B), Fig. 24.7. Stick a length of gummed tape over each joint (C); you will find that slight trimming at the edges will be needed when the squares are assembled as at (A). You can do this on a shooting board, pressing down on a flat piece of wood placed on top of the veneers to stop them wrinkling. It's advisable to put the veneers together dry on the actual top, the latter being marked out in squares as shown at (A). They are again taped together.

The actual veneering is by the caul method – unless you have a press available. Veneer the front and back simultaneously, and assuming you are employing cauls, you will need to use several pairs of cross-bearers slightly bowed in length so that pressure is applied at the centre first, driving the glue out at the edges. Although you can use a modern synthetic adhesive, Scotch glue is recommended because if anything should go wrong you can easily rectify it by warming the glue slightly to re-liquefy it.

EDGING THE TOP

Once the glue has set, trim the edges square all round. To work the grooves for the tongues, the most effective way is to use a portable powered router fitted with a deep fence so that you can hold it upright without difficulty. Theoretically, the edges are grooved with the same setting as the plywood, but in practice it is advisable to alter it slightly so that the lipping stands up a trifle proud – this enables it to be levelled afterwards with the minimum amount being removed from the veneer.

The edging is mitred round three sides of each main top, and a ½in lipping screwed on at the closing edges. In the case of the leaf, only the short ends have a wide lipping. Note that the groove for the tongue is continued a short way along each mitre, but remember that the shape has to be worked and the corners rounded.

If you have a bandsaw you can use it to cut the basic overall shape. Otherwise, you can employ an ordinary handsaw to make the straight cuts, planing the shape afterwards. Fig. 24.2 gives a section through the edging and this can be planed in its entirety. Level the surface with a finely-set smoothing plane and follow on with a scraper; finish off with glasspaper, the sequence of use being Middle 2, 1½, and Flour grades. However, if you have one, an orbital sander is ideal as it can cope with the varying direction of the grain.

SLIDING ACTION OF TOPS

To ensure that the slides are parallel and in the correct positions, the tops are laid face down on the floor, and the framework placed in the exact position. The slides, which should be free from undue friction without being slack, are placed over the tops, held

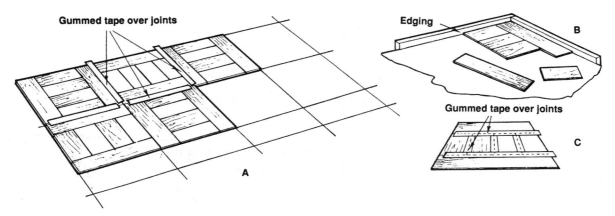

Fig. 24.7. How the veneers are prepared for laying.

close to the bearers, and fixed with two screws each. The remaining screws are added after testing that the sliding action is all it should be. A gap of about 1¼in is left between the ends of the slides, and stops are later screwed beneath the bearers as in Fig. 24.6. These stops ensure that the tops are about central when closed.

To prevent the tops from being pulled right out, spring stops are let in beneath as in Fig. 24.4. Cut recesses in the tops to take them, and slope one end slightly so that the piece of ⅛in hardwood which forms the spring stands up about ⅛in. It hits against the end rail when the top is pulled out; by pressing it in, however, the top can be slid right out when required. Both main tops and leaf have four dowels let in to ensure exact location.

LEAF SHELF
This is a piece of plywood screwed beneath two stretchers as in Fig. 24.6. Also, notches are cut in the end rails to take the stretchers which are screwed up. There should be about ¼in clearance beneath the rails for the leaf.

Probably the best finish would be a polyurethane lacquer which would withstand most of the hazards such tables are subjected to.

CUTTING LIST

	INCHES			*MM*		
	L	W	T	L	W	T
4 legs	30	2½	2¼	762	64	58
2 rails	37	4¾	⅞	940	121	22
2 rails	28	4¾	⅞	711	121	22
2 bearers	37	2¾	⅞	940	70	22
4 slides	20½	2¾	⅞	521	70	22
2 stretchers	37	2½	⅞	940	64	22
1 shelf	18	15¼	¼	458	388	6
2 tops	32¼	20¼	¾	819	514	19
1 leaf	32¼	12¼	¾	819	311	19
2 lippings	37½	2¼	⅞	953	58	22
4 lippings	23	2¼	⅞	584	58	22
2 lippings	13½	2¼	⅞	343	58	22
4 lippings	33	⅞	½	838	23	13

Working allowances have been made to lengths and widths; thicknesses are net.

SIDEBOARD IN TEAK

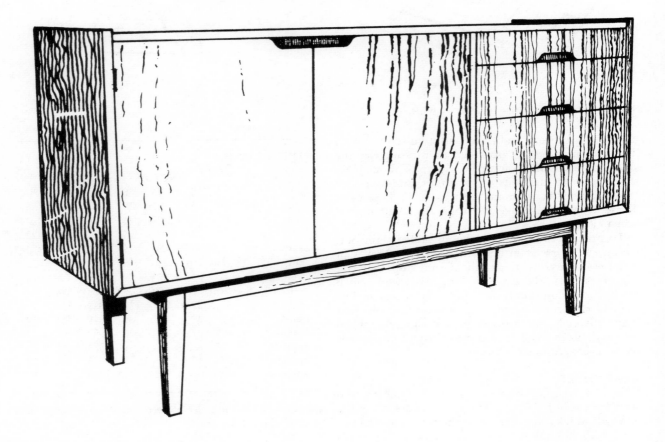

One side of this sideboard contains four drawers, the other side having two doors enclosing a storage compartment with a shelf; the storage section is supported by an underframe with tapered legs. The overall dimensions are 60in long by 18in wide by 34in high, and all show wood is veneered in teak.

The carcase is constructed on a base measuring 60in by 18in, and has a storage compartment with two doors on the left side and a compartment on the right containing four drawers; it is made from ¾in laminated board which is veneered on the face with teak and on the reverse side with a balancer veneer such as obeche. The width of the drawers is 21¾in, and the top one has a depth of 3¼in while the other three are 5⅜in. There is a plywood back ¼in thick running the whole length of the carcase.

CARCASE

The laminated board for this is cut to a width of 14in and lipped with solid teak, 2in wide; the top and bottom members of the carcase are lipped on both edges. The two ends are lipped on all four sides with the top corners mitred, the central member being lipped on the sides only. The lippings are fixed with tongues, ¾in by ³⁄₁₆in, inserted into grooves and bonded with a PVA adhesive.

VENEERING

After all the lippings have been glued on, the boards are cleaned down and veneered; the base is veneered on the inside only at this stage.

The veneer is prepared by cutting the leaves to length, allowing 1in extra length for cleaning up. The edges are straightened up by planing them on a long shooting board, and the leaves joined together by sticking glued brown paper tape along the joints; don't be tempted to use a pressure-sensitive tape as when it is pulled off it can easily bring slivers of veneer with it.

The method of bonding the veneer is to apply a PVA adhesive to both the board and the veneer and then to put them into a veneer press. But if a press is not available, it can be laid by the hammer method, using Scotch glue.

JOINTS

The top of the sideboard is joined to the end members by a ⁷⁄₁₆in by ⅜in tongue which is cut on the top member, and a ⅜in deep groove cut into the end members, stopping ½in from the front edge to give a vertical edge joint. The top is also recessed ⅜in down from the top edge of the ends.

Stopped housing joints are used to fix the central vertical member to the carcase top and base, the bottom one being glued and screwed from underneath.

The base of the carcase is joined to the ends by a lapped joint which runs up to the lippings which are

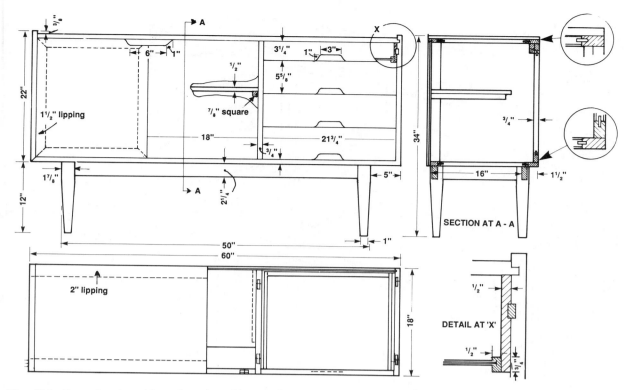

Fig. 25.1. Front elevation; side section; plan with part of top removed; also drawer detail.

joined at the corners of the carcase by secret mitred dovetails. The bottom teak veneer can be laid after the sides and bottom have been bonded together.

The back is a ¼in thick panel of plywood veneered with mahogany on the inside and grooved into the top and sides; it extends below the base to the bottom edge of the carcase and is fixed with screws from the back.

DRAWER CONSTRUCTION

The drawer fronts are made from 1in African mahogany, the top edge being lipped, and the front veneered with teak. The sides and back are all made from ½in African mahogany.

The sides are joined to the front by lapped dovetails and to the back by through dovetails. Slips are glued on the bottom edges of the drawer sides. They are ¾in by ½in and are grooved to take a ¼in mahogany plywood drawer bottom which slides in from the back into a groove which is cut into the inner face of the drawer front. When the drawer bottom is in position it is screwed up into the drawer back.

There are ¾in by ³⁄₁₆in grooves cut into the drawer sides. These grooves are stopped 3in from the front, and slide upon ¾in by ½in drawer runners which are housed and screwed into the carcase sides; the runners also stop 3in from the front of the sideboard and act as stops.

The recessed handle for each drawer is cut out of the bottom edge of the drawer front to a depth of ⅝in; the shape of the face can be seen from the drawing, and the drawer is, of course, opened by the fingers pulling from underneath.

DOORS

The storage compartment has two doors which are made from laminated board veneered with teak on

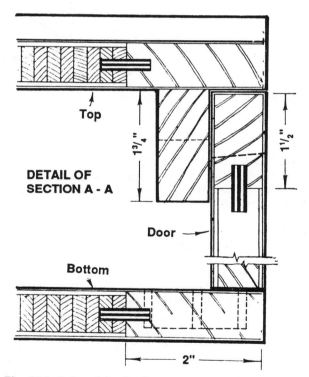

Fig. 25.2. Enlarged details of Section A-A showing top, doors, and bottom; note the lippings.

the outside and mahogany on the inside, in the same way as the ends. The lipping is mitred on the outside top corner and on the inside edge, 1in down from the top where, as can be seen from the drawing, the handle is cut out. The handle is shaped out and has a small bevel sloping back from the top edge, so that the doors can be opened by the fingers pulling from the top. The doors are hung on 2in brass butts, and there is a shaped door stop which is screwed up into the top behind the handle openings.

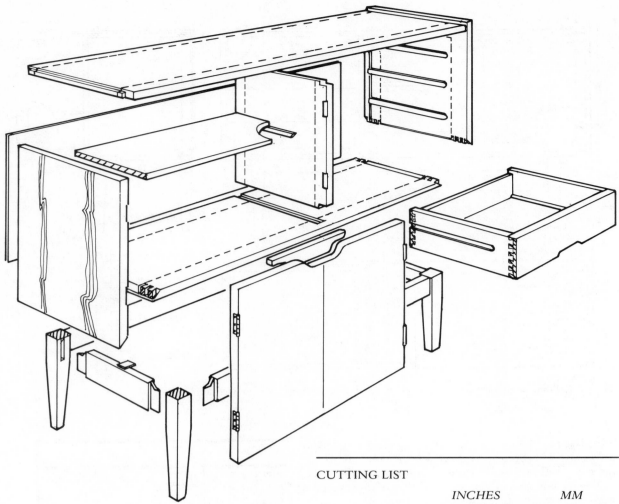

Fig. 25.3. Exploded view of construction.

STORAGE COMPARTMENT

This is 36in wide, and contains a loose shelf resting upon two pieces fixed to the vertical members with brass screws and screw cups.

LEGS

The carcase is supported by an underframe 50in by 16in which consists of four legs joined by rails. The legs are 12in long by 1⅞in square, and are tapered down to 1in square at the toes; the taper begins 9in from the bottom of the legs. The frame rails are 2¼in by ⅞in in section and are set back ¼in from the face of the legs.

The rails and legs are joined with mortise and tenon joints. The tenons have secret haunches, and their ends are mitred to meet their partners inside the mortises in the legs.

Solid teak is used for the underframe, and it is advisable to de-grease the joints before bonding them with PVA adhesive.

The frame is screwed to the carcase through six small brass plates which are recessed into the rails.

FINISH

If teak is used for the sideboard it is best to give the wood an oil finish, as this brings out the rich colour of the wood and the proprietary brands of Teak Oil are most effective.

CUTTING LIST

	INCHES			MM		
	L	W	T	L	W	T
Carcase						
1 top★	60	14¼	¾	1524	362	19
1 bottom★	60½	13¾	¾	1536	349	19
4 lippings	60½	2¼	¾	1536	58	19
2 ends★	18½	14¼	¾	470	362	19
4 lippings	22½	2¼	¾	572	58	19
4 lippings	18½	2¼	¾	470	58	19
1 partition★	22	14¼	¾	559	362	19
2 lippings	22	2¼	¾	559	58	19
2 doors★	15½	18	¾	394	457	19
4 lippings	18½	1¾	¾	470	45	19
4 lippings	21	1¾	¾	533	45	19
1 back, ply	60	21	¼	1524	533	6
1 shelf	36½	13¼	½	927	336	13
Drawers						
1 front	22¼	3½	⅞	565	89	22
3 fronts	22¼	5⅞	⅞	565	150	22
2 sides	18	3½	½	457	89	13
6 sides	18	5⅞	½	457	150	13
1 back	22¼	3	½	565	76	13
3 backs	22¼	5½	½	565	140	13
4 bottoms, ply	20¾	17	¼	527	432	6
Stool underframe						
4 legs	12½	2¼	2	318	58	51
2 rails	50	2½	⅞	1269	64	22
2 rails	15½	2½	⅞	394	64	22

Note:– items marked ★ can be particle board.
Working allowances have been made to lengths and widths; thicknesses are net.

EXTENDING DINING TABLE WITH LOOSE LEAF

The closed size of this table is a convenient 45in by 33in, which can be extended by means of a loose leaf to 60in; the leaf is 15in wide and is stored under the table top when not in use.

GENERAL REMARKS

The sizes for setting out and enlarged details are given in Figs 26.1 and 26.2.

You have a choice in regard to the tops, namely (a) the use of ready-veneered blockboard, with solid moulded lippings tongued on around the edges; or (b) employing solid timber with the edges moulded to the required profile.

From the point of view of stability, the first alternative is probably better, bearing in mind the need of perfectly true surfaces for sliding, but if you can obtain prime well-seasoned and figured timber it could be used with advantage.

Note, however, that the cutting list allows for one sheet of veneered blockboard to be sawn in half for the two tops; using solid timber will mean, therefore, that you will have to alter the sizes and omit the lippings.

But to avoid using veneers, it is best to utilise solid figured timber for the frame rails, particularly as mitred and dovetailed joints are recommended for the corners.

LEGS

These run from the underside of the top to the floor. Commence to turn them from immediately below the frame rails, thus leaving squares of 2⅛in at the tops. Also, taper them from 2⅛in dia at the rails to 1⅜in diameter at the break of the toes, which are formed by reducing the diameter by ⅛in at a height of 4½in, while maintaining the same line of taper.

Fix the position of the legs in the frame, by working back two faces of each square back by ⅛in, as shown in Fig. 26.3. You can, however, omit this refinement if you wish by taking the squares straight up through. Again, if you prefer square tapered legs instead of turned ones, you can follow the same procedure.

FRAME RAILS (B) AND (C)

Start by cutting the mitred and dovetailed joints as in Fig. 26.4. Alternatively you could use mitred and tongued joints, or through-dovetailing, but these will involve using veneer to hide the joints.

Next, slot the end rails so that the slides can pass through. Now you will have to decide whether to dovetail the cross rails (F) up to the lengthwise rails, or slot them in and screw them.

Glue and cramp the frame rails together and leave to set. Meanwhile, you can prepare the sockets and the screw holes in the squares of the legs, working two on each face and staggering them to miss each other.

Now you can fix the legs to the frame rails, gluing and screwing both ways to provide an effective bracing; follow on by inserting the cross rails that carry the loose leaf.

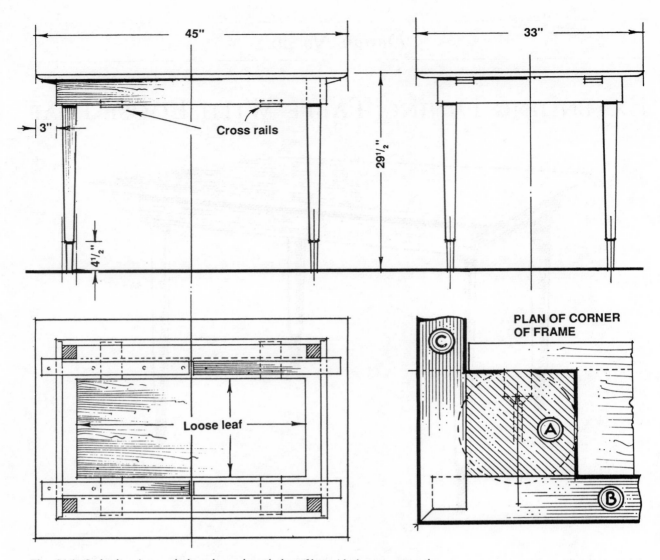

45"

33"

3"

29½"

4½"

Cross rails

Loose leaf

PLAN OF CORNER
OF FRAME

C

A

B

Fig. 26.1. Scale elevations and plan; also, enlarged plan of leg with the top removed.

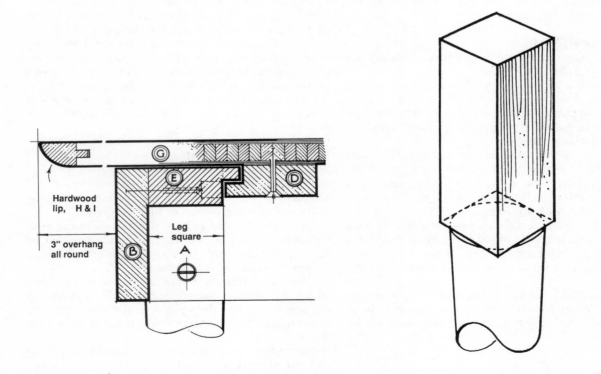

Hardwood
lip,   H & I

3" overhang
all round

G

E

D

Leg
square

A

B

Fig. 26.2. Enlarged section through the top and frame.

Fig. 26.3. Detail of the top of the leg.

92

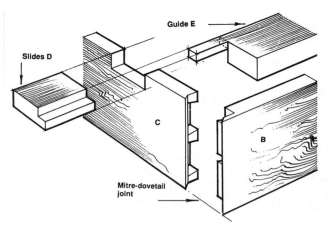

Fig. 26.4. Construction of framework and slides.

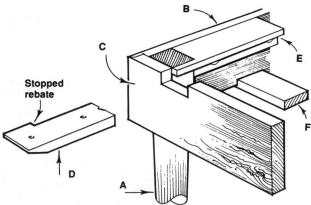

Fig. 26.5. How the slides fit into the guides.

SLIDES AND GUIDES (D) AND (E)

You need to rebate the edges of these so that they slide one into the other as shown in the details in Figs. 26.1, 26.4 and 26.5. Stop the rebates on the slides at the inside of the frame rails; those on the guides run right through, however. The latter should be fitted around the leg squares and then you can glue and screw them to the frame rails. Clean off the top surfaces of the rails to ensure that the tops run smoothly. Now bevel off the ends of the slides and prepare the screw holes for fixing them to the tops later. It's preferable to use slot-screwing only for attaching them (without glue) if the tops are of solid timber, as this will accommodate any movement that might occur. And, of course, you should select true and even grained stuff for both the slides and the guides to make sure that they slide easily; rubbing wax or candle grease on the edges will help, too.

TOPS AND LEAF (ITEMS G TO K)

If you are using veneered blockboard, keep the one piece (G) in the cutting list intact until after you have tongued and glued on the lippings all round. The idea is to complete the top as one unit, 45¼in long, and then cut it into two halves with as fine a saw as you have (a planer saw blade would be ideal). This will, of course, preserve the continuity and matching of the grain of the veneer across the tops.

As the first step, therefore, square up the edges of the blockboard and groove it all round for the tongues of the lippings; glue and cramp these on, mitering the corners. When the glue has set you can work the moulded profile all round the edges.

Be very careful when cleaning up the top face afterwards to avoid breaking through the veneer, and then saw the blockboard into two equal pieces. Naturally, the sawn edges will need to be shot true with a finely-set plane, and when this is done you can glue locating dowels into one edge to enter matching holes in the other – it helps to make these holes slightly oversize.

FITTING THE SLIDES

To obtain the position for the slides of the tops, temporarily fix the latter to the table frame in its correct place with G-cramps and arrange a 3in overhang all round. Invert the table and accurately mark from the slots cut in the end rails; then remove the tops and carry the markings lengthwise along them in the form of gauge lines. When gluing and screwing the slides in place, allow a slight tolerance to facilitate an easy action, but not to the extent of allowing any side-to-side chatter.

If you are fitting the loose leaf as suggested, make an alteration in the cutting list to include this as one piece together with that for the two tops – this will ensure the same graining of veneer. Thus, the piece of veneered blockboard for the two tops plus one leaf would read approximately 63in by 33in.

Using solid timber means that you will probably need to match and joint separate boards to obtain the necessary widths of the tops and the leaf. As already mentioned, the slides should be slot-screwed in place without glue; you will probably find that the loose leaf will need battens to stop it winding and, if so, they should also be fixed by slot-screwing and no glue.

CUTTING LIST

Part	INCHES			MM		
	L	W	T	L	W	T
A 4 legs	30	2¼	2⅛	762	57	54
B 2 frame rails	40	4¼	⅞	1016	108	22
C 2 frame rails	28	4¼	⅞	711	108	22
D 4 slides	22	3	⅞	558	706	22
E 2 guides	39	3	1⅛	990	706	29
F 2 cross rails	28	3½	⅞	711	89	22
G 2 tops from 1 piece	33	45	¾	838	1143	19
H 2 lippings	48	2	¾	1219	51	19
I 2 lippings	36	2	¾	914	51	19
J 1 leaf	33	16	¾	838	407	19
K 2 lippings	18	2	¾	457	51	19

Working allowances have been made to lengths and widths; thicknesses are net.

SCULPTURED TEA WAGON

This design breaks away from the conventional 'four-corner-posts-hospital-type-trolley' and by using stopped mortise and tenon joints mitred at the shoulders, the free curves on the side frames produce a sculptured look.

To achieve the necessary shape, the side frames have to be made from fairly wide pieces of timber, but the offcuts from the shaping need not be wasted, as they could be handy for making laminated lamps and bowls.

CONSTRUCTION

Make up each side frame (front leg, back leg, top rail, and bottom rail), marking them out in pairs.

1 Prepare the timber to the sizes shown in the cutting list.

2 Note that the mortises are set back ⅝in from the edge of the wood and parallel to it, Fig. 27.1. Mark out the mitres and gauge both sides to meet them. Remove the waste wood and finish to the line, using a wide shoulder plane.

3 Mark out the mortises and tenons. You may prefer to cut the mortises before stage 2, or you may find it easier to cut the mortises after the mitres have been cut, as there is less likelihood of damage to the edges of the mortises. Note also that the shoulders of the tenon on the back leg and the rear of the bottom rail are set at 85 degrees, see Fig. 27.6, No 2.

4 Cut the mortises in the top rail, the back leg, and the front leg.

5 Saw tenons on the back leg and the bottom rail. Fit the respective joints carefully and trim the shoulders and mitres if necessary with a shoulder plane.

6 Assemble both side frames dry and check for exact matching, one on top of the other. As the frames are right- and left-handed, choose the inside surface of each and mark each member clearly. Mark out the centres for the dowel joints (Fig. 27.3) on one frame and transfer these positions to the other frame in pairs.

7 Use a ⅜in dia Forstner bit for the holes to a depth of ⅝in.

8 Prepare the cross rails to exact length.

9 Groove the cross rails, the bottom rails and the

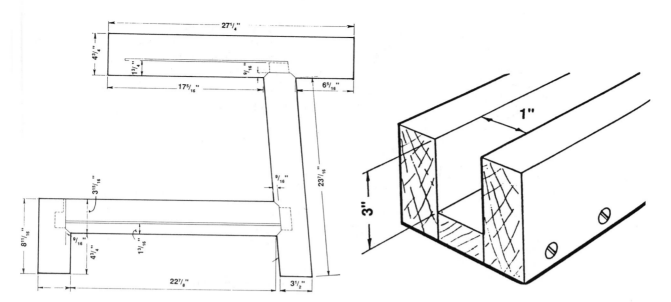

Fig. 27.1. Elevation showing joint positions and ¼in grooves.

Fig. 27.2. Jig for trimming gauge lines.

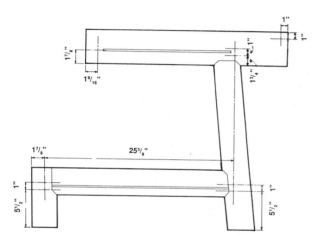

Fig. 27.3. Elevation showing positions of dowel centres.

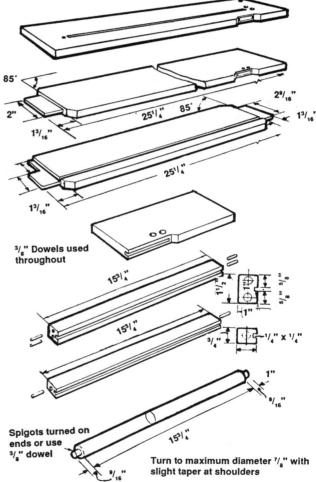

³/₈" Dowels used throughout

Spigots turned on ends or use ³/₈" dowel

Turn to maximum diameter ⁷/₈" with slight taper at shoulders

Fig. 27.5. Processing details.

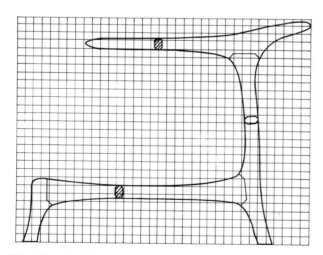

Fig. 27.4. Final shape drawn on 1 inch squared grid.

top rails using a power router and a ¼in cutter to a depth of ¼in. Note that the groove is stopped at both ends on the top rails, Fig. 27.3.

10 Mark out and drill the ends of the cross rails, using a ³/₈in drill to a depth of 1⅜in.

11 Glue the side frames, checking that they are not in winding, and leave to set.

12 Make the templates to the shape shown in Fig. 27.4, using stout cardboard.

13 Clean up both faces of the side frames. Draw round the templates and cut to shape with a bandsaw or a portable jigsaw.

14 Clean up the edges; a spokeshave is good for this plus a rasp where the rails meet the legs. Slightly

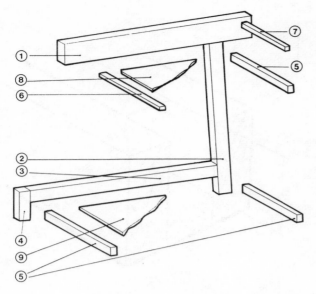

Fig. 27.6. Exploded drawing; numbered parts relate to process-ing and cutting lists.

curve all edges of the side frames and the cross rails (³/₁₆in).

15 Cut the dowelling to length (2in), and glue into the cross rails.

16 Turn the spigot ends on the handle.

17 Prepare the plywood shelves to size. Have a trial cramping-up to ensure that the dowelled joints go together and that the plywood fits properly.

18 Drill for the castors; note that the holes are drilled off-centre.

19 Glasspaper all parts and finish with teak oil or your own choice of polish.

20 Glue and cramp the cross rails and the handle to the side frames, but do not put glue on the plywood or in the grooves. Make sure that the wagon stands four square on a level surface.

21 Fit the castors according to type.

CUTTING LIST

		INCHES			MM		
Part		L	W	T	L	W	T
1	2 top rails	27¾	5	1	705	127	25
2	2 back legs	25¾	3¾	1	654	95	25
3	2 bottom rails	26⅞	4¼	1	683	108	25
4	2 front legs	9⅛	3¾	1	232	95	25
5	3 cross rails	16¼	1¾	1	413	44	25
6	1 top front cross rail	16¼	1	1	413	25	25
7	1 handle	18¼	1¼	1	463	32	25
8	1 top shelf, ply	19	16⅜	¼	482	416	6
9	1 bottom shelf, ply	25½	16⅜	¼	648	416	6

Working allowances have been made to lengths and widths; thicknesses are net.

PROCESSING LIST FOR PARTS IN FIG. 27.6:

Part 1:— cut mortise for back leg; drill four holes; plough stopped groove.

Part 2:— cut mortise for bottom rail; saw tenon for top rail; drill two holes.

Part 3:— saw tenons for front and back legs; plough groove ¼in by ¼in (6mm by 6mm).

Part 4:— cut mortise for bottom rail; drill two holes.

Part 5:— drill two holes ⁵/₁₆in (9mm) dia by 1⅜in (35mm) deep in each end of cross rail; plough groove.

Part 6:— drill one hole ⁵/₁₆in (9mm) dia by 1⅜in (35mm) deep in each end of cross rail; plough groove.

Part 7:— turn on lathe to a suitable diameter with a curved taper to the shoulders.

DINING TABLE WITH AUTOMATIC RISING CENTRAL LEAF

This table will seat four people when closed and six when extended. The leaf rises automatically, the mechanism being entirely of wood. The half top A shown in the plan, Fig. 28.1 operates the opening; the other half of the main top B, Fig. 28.1, must be pulled out first, thus uncovering the leaf and releasing the lopers of A. The latter, when withdrawn, operate the levers which raise the leaf to the level of the main top.

Both tops are then pushed up to the leaf for use as an extended table. To drop the leaf and close the table, top B is drawn away a little from the leaf which lowers it and this enables both halves of the main top to be closed. It sounds rather complicated, but you will find it quite simple to operate. A is automatically locked until B is drawn well out away from the centre.

CONSTRUCTION

Make the legs C from 2½in square stuff and mortise them for the tenoned frieze rails D and E, Fig. 28.2. Taper the legs on the inside faces only from below the rails to 1¼in square at the bottom, and round off the outside corners as shown in the enlarged section, Fig. 28.1; all the other edges should be softened to a pencil-round with glasspaper. You will need to cut the frieze rails D away centrally, allowing for the leaf thickness plus the baize or felt cloth beneath the main tops.

Notch the end frieze rails E for the lopers G which carry the main tops. Note that the lopers to the half B of the top are closer together than for the half A, (see plan, Fig. 28.1) so the notches must be cut accordingly. It is a good idea to fit the centre cross rail F by means of a slip-dovetail housing to the frieze rails D. Assemble the underframing dry and use a straightedge across all rails to mark the positions of the notches, working to the loper thickness. Square the lines down.

To prevent the lopers from rising, add the fillets S, screwing them to the bottom edge in pairs and cutting through the rails for the fillets to pass (Fig. 28.2). After you have cut away for the lopers, you can glue the underframing together, adding glue blocks to all the joints at the legs for extra strength; see Fig. 28.1.

TOPS AND LEAF

Use good, dry material for these if they are to be solid wood. Veneered blockboard or plywood, ¾in thick, would be preferable but you would have to lip or veneer the edges; one way would be to bend thin strips of flexible wood round which could be glued and pinned in place.

Now turn the framing upside down, place the lopers and the tops into the closed position, and screw through the lopers into the tops. Screw the

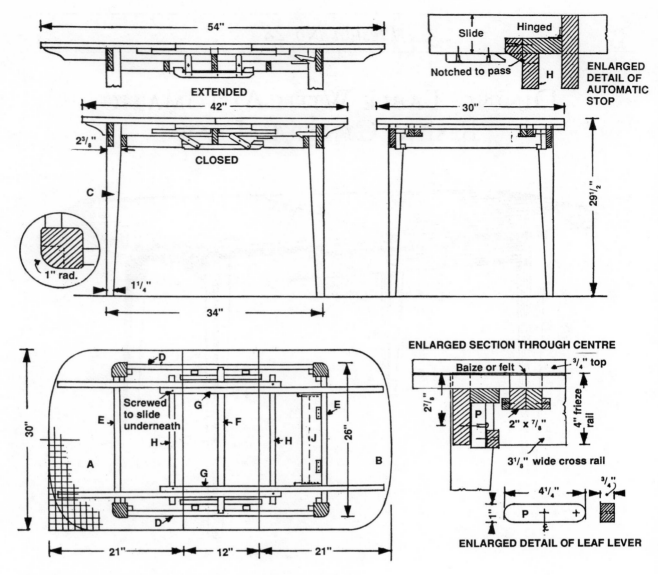

Fig. 28.1. Side and end sectional elevations, plan, and enlarged details.

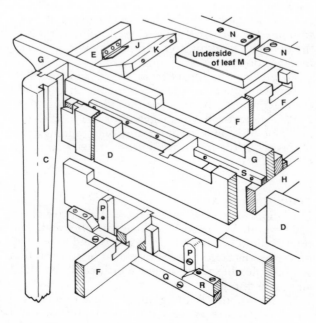

Fig. 28.2 Cut-away view showing action of table.

battens N to the leaf, Fig. 28.2, open the tops, and add the leaf, closing tightly together. The leaf-raising mechanism can then be added.

LEAF RAISERS

On each side of the table this assembly consists of two levers, P, Fig. 28.1, connected by an arm Q at the bottom, Fig. 28.2. The arm is attached to the levers with bolts and nuts or with roundhead screws with washers under their heads and between the lever and the arm, and they must work freely. Add small blocks at each end of the arms to connect with the stops screwed to the lopers, as in the plan, Fig. 28.1. When you have completed the mechanism, screw it to the inside of the frieze rails D with the levers in a vertical position as shown in Fig. 28.1. (extended table).

SELF-LOCKING DEVICE

This is shown in Fig. 28.2 and fits freely between the inner lopers. Use old hinges that open freely to enable the stop to drop by its own weight; otherwise it should be pivoted to drilled metal brackets attached to the frieze rail. Projecting stops screwed to the underside of the inner lopers raise the device when pulled out, thus releasing the stop rail screwed to the outer lopers attached to top A.

Finish all working parts glass-smooth and add a little graphite to ensure easy working. Plot part of the D–ended top from the 1in squares on the plan, Fig. 28.1. Glue baize or cloth strips under those parts of the tops which cover the leaf to avoid scratching the surfaces. This type of furniture looks well lightly stained and wax polished, but would respond equally well to a polyester lacquer finish.

CUTTING LIST

Part	INCHES			MM		
	L	W	T	L	W	T
C 4 legs	29½	2⅝	2⅜	749	67	61
D 2 frieze rails	32½	4¼	⅞	825	108	22
E 2 frieze rails	24½	4¼	⅞	622	108	22
F 1 cross rail	25¼	3½	⅞	641	89	22
G 4 lopers	35½	2¼	⅞	902	58	22

CUTTING LIST (continued)

	INCHES			MM		
	L	W	T	L	W	T
H 2 stops	22½	2¼	⅞	571	58	22
J 1 locking rail	16½	2½	⅞	419	64	22
K 1 piece for locking rail	16½	1⅝	⅞	419	42	22
L 2 tops	30½	27¼	¾	775	692	19
M 1 leaf	30½	12¼	¾	775	311	19
N 4 leaf battens	9½	1¾	¾	242	45	19
P 4 levers	4¾	1¼	¾	121	32	19
Q 2 arms	13	1¼	¾	330	32	19
R 4 blocks from 1 piece	9	1	¾	229	25	19
S 4 fillets	35½	¾	⅜	902	19	10
T 2 finger pulls	16½	1¼	¾	419	32	19

Working allowance have been made to lengths and widths; thicknesses are net.

SIDEBOARD WITH TAMBOUR-FRONTED CUPBOARDS

This very elegant sideboard is made of solid English walnut throughout; not many of us are likely to be the fortunate possessors of this kind of timber, but the design could equally well be made up in a veneered blockboard, although the tambours, of course, would have to be made from solid stuff.

MARKING AND CUTTING OUT

The first step is to mark out the cabinet top and bottom. You will see that the total amount of 'swell' on the front edge is 1⅜in; probably the best way to get a sweet curve is to bend a thin strip of wood to the required curve, and ask a helper to pencil in the line.

After you have cut and trimmed these to size and shape, there is the problem of marking and routing out the ¼in by ¼in channel for the tambours. If you have a portable electric router, the job is a straight-forward exercise of making up the requisite fences or jigs and routing out the channel. Otherwise, you will need to make a scratch stock or a hand router, using both in conjunction with a chisel.

Next, mark and cut the two ends to size. The joints at the top corner are secret mitre dovetails, Fig. 29.2A, and at the bottom corners, lapped dovetails, B, 29.2, and you can cut these now. However, note that a through rebate is cut along the back edge of each piece, and a similar one is cut on the back of the

upper edge (only) of the top, this latter one being stopped ¼in short at each end. The rebate size is ½in by ½in and its purpose is to accept the frame.

Obviously, the channels for the tambours must be identical in both the top and the bottom, and to ensure this, it is definitely worthwhile making a template out of tracing paper and tracing the curve through with carbon paper; you will see from Fig. 29.1 that the channel is set back ¼in from the front edge.

More work on the top and bottom pieces consists of cutting dovetail housings for the panels which mask the tambours, and mortises to accept the tenons on the drawer partitions; in addition, the tenons on the bottom of this partition are wedged.

STOOL SECTION

Dealing now with the stool section, the first stage is to mark out, cut, and shape the legs, which have their arrises rounded to the section shown. Follow on by marking and cutting out the two long stretcher rails, and remember that they taper towards their centres – again, these will need shaping to section. The short end rails are haunch-tenoned into the legs, and can be prepared next; don't forget to channel a groove ¼in by ¼in, and ⅜in away from the top edge, to engage the fixing buttons, and this groove can run right through.

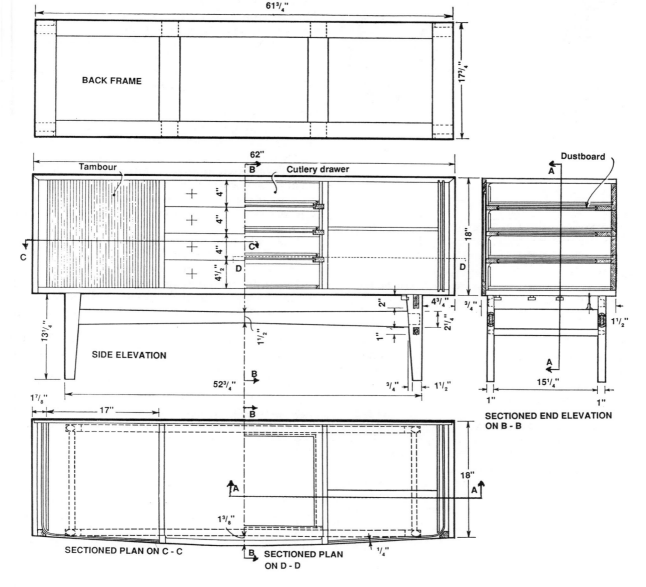

Fig. 29.1. Elevation, plans, and sections.

You can next mark out and joint up the back frame. As you will see from Fig. 29.1, this is an uncomplicated mortise–and–tenon job, and all the tenons can be through tenons as all edges (except the bottom) are covered. The ¼in by ¼in grooves for the panels can be run the full length of the rails and stiles without being stopped. A point to note is that the panels themselves are 'fielded', that is, the thickness of the panel is tapered away around the edges. Although it is obviously unwise to do this with man-made boards, it is worthwhile taking the trouble with solid stuff to avoid splits occurring through possible shrinkage; for the same reason solid panels should be inserted dry without being glued.

DRAWER MATERIAL
Moving on to the preparation of the drawer stuff, you will see that provision has been made for (optional) dustboards under the three top drawers. In addition to making the mortise and tenon joints on the drawer rails and runners, if you want the dustboards you will need to work a ³⁄₁₆in by ³⁄₁₆in groove centrally on the inside of each member, stopping it 1¹⁄₁₆in short of each end in the case of the front and back rails.

The drawer fronts and sides are dovetailed

together, as is common practice, but before doing this, prepare all the parts, bearing in mind that the bottom drawer is deeper than the others.

Cut the parts to size, and cut the groove in the back of each drawer front for its drawer bottom. When you have done this, mark up the front and sides for dovetailing, making sure that you mark the dovetails so that the bottom one covers the end groove, which would otherwise show as a gap. Lastly, make up the drawer slip.

MAKING THE TAMBOURS
Making up the tambour doors is rather a tedious business, but is greatly helped if you have access to a circular saw and a spindle moulder; and a circular saw is essential to do the job accurately.

If you cannot use a spindle moulder for one reason or another, the best plan is to obtain your timber, which should be a piece 37in long, 17in wide, and planed to finish ³⁄₁₆in thick. You will need a moulding cutter or a scratch stock profiled to the style of moulding you require (Fig. 29.2), and this is worked along the edge of the board each time before parting off a strip ³⁄₈in wide by means of the saw.

One other method is available and that is to buy

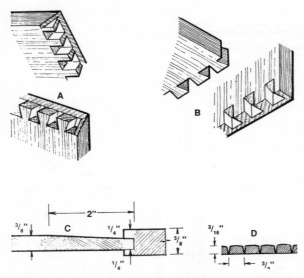

Fig. 29.2. (A) secret mitre dovetail joint at top and end; (B) lapped dovetail joint at bottom and end; (C) detail of fielded panels in back; (D) section of tambour.

strips of plain moulding of the requisite section, using a scratch stock or a moulding plane on these to produce the tambours; if you have a router table on which you can invert a power router, this could also be used to mould the edges.

LAYING THE TAMBOURS

You will need two pieces of good quality sail canvas or a similar material to form the backing for the tambours, and this should be cut ½in shorter than the length of the tambours; this means you will need two pieces each 18½in by 16in. Stretch the pieces taut on a baseboard such as a piece of chipboard or multiply; apply a liberal coating of glue and lay the tambour strips on their backs in position. This means (a) that the top and bottom quarter-inch of each tambour is clear of the canvas and consequently left unglued, so that the canvas does not foul the channel; and (b) you will need to make a simple jig from two thin strips of scrapwood fixed to the baseboard to form a right angle.

Take care that the tambour strips do not stick together during the process – the best way to do this is to give each strip a coat of white polish first, making sure that none gets on to the back of the strips.

When the glue has set, try the tambours in the grooves, and you may find a touch of paraffin wax will help them run sweetly. To polish them, remove them from the cabinet and roll them round a suitably-sized cylinder, such as an old glue tin or something similar.

ASSEMBLY

When assembling, you will probably find the best way is to put the job up dry first before gluing up. Knock up the back frame and panels, checking for squareness; this is most important at this juncture, as this assembly virtually determines whether the finished job is square.

Next, fit the ends to the bottom, and put the back frame into position. Follow this by positioning the masking panels, the drawer partitions, and the drawer rails and runners. Fit on the tambour panels, and position the top on to the assembly.

ASSEMBLING THE STOOL

This is straightforward and calls for no special instructions. Having put it together, dry, offer it up to the cabinet to determine the exact position and sizes for the buttons, and also bore a hole for the single screw at each end which is screwed into the cabinet bottom (see Fig. 29.1)

DRAWERS AND SHELVES

On this design, the top drawer was divided into nine compartments for cutlery etc, but of course you can amend this to suit your own requirements. Similarly, a shelf was fitted in each cupboard, resting on three small dowels corresponding with holes in the tambour masking and drawer division. A set of holes was drilled at three different levels to give shelf adjustment.

When you have made the final adjustments, you can proceed with the actual glasspapering and gluing up. Follow the procedure outlined above, but don't forget to put the tambour panels in position before fixing the top! Both the tambour and the masking panels should be fed in from the back before gluing up.

You will also have to glue up and assemble the drawers, leaving the fronts flat and planing them down in position.

Our design was finished with three coats of white (clear) French polish, rubbing down lightly between each coat, and giving the resulting coating a wax finish.

CUTTING LIST

	INCHES			MM		
	L	W	T	L	W	T
1 top	62½	20	⅝	1587	508	16
1 bottom	62	19¼	⅝	1575	489	16
2 ends	18½	18½	⅝	470	470	16
2 partitions	18¼	19⅛	⅝	464	485	16
4 legs	13¾	2½	1	349	64	25
2 long stretchers	52½	2½	1	1333	64	25
2 short stretchers	17¼	1¼	¾	438	32	19
2 stool end rails	17¼	2¼	¾	438	57	19
2 masking panels	17½	17	⅜	445	431	10
2 back panel rails	62	2¾	⅝	1575	70	16
4 back panel stiles	18¼	3¼	⅝	464	83	16
2 back panels	14	16¼	⅜	356	413	10
1 back panel	20	16¼	⅜	508	413	10
3 drawer fronts	24¼	4⅜	1	611	111	25
1 drawer front	24¼	4¾	1	611	121	25
6 drawer sides	18½	3¾	⅜	470	95	10
2 drawer sides	18½	4¾	⅜	470	121	10
3 drawer backs	23¼	2¾	⅜	590	70	10
1 drawer back	23¼	3¾	⅜	590	95	10
4 drawer bottoms	23	18¼	¼	584	464	6
2 shelves	17	10¼	⅜	432	260	10
2 shelf bearers	17	1¾	⅜	432	45	10
4 shelf bearers	10½	1¾	⅜	267	45	10
3 dustboards	22¼	14¾	3/16	565	375	5
3 front drawer rails	24¼	2½	⅝	611	64	16
3 back drawer rails	24¼	1⅛	⅝	611	29	16
6 drawer runners	16	1½	⅝	407	38	16
8 drawer slips	18½	¾	½	470	19	13
2 tambour guides	17¼	1½	1	438	38	25
98 tambour strips	17	⅝	3/16	432	16	5

Working allowances have been made to lengths and widths; thicknesses are net.

Easy-to-make Dinner Wagon

This is a fairly simple and straightforward piece to make up from the practical point of view, its main features being the trays which are faced with a plastic laminate, and from a design standpoint the broad end rails with the handles shaped from the solid.

The original was made in teak and given a matt finish, and the plastic laminate was also teak grained. Most hardwoods would, of course, be suitable, although it is better to think in terms of matching the wood to the plastic laminate available, rather than the other way round.

CONSTRUCTION

Prepare all the material to size, and mark out all the joints except the top end rails as it is better to deal with these later, the arrangements of the joints being somewhat non-standard in more ways than one!

To gain the maximum size possible, haunched tenons have only been used where essential, that is, where the top edges of the rails are rounded. For the same reason, the tenon has been arranged slightly off centre, and the rebate then made to line up with the tenon.

Now cut and fit all the joints. Although the tenon

at the top is subsequently cut into to form part of the mortise for the end rail, you can fit it as normal at this stage.

The rebates for the trays are ⅜in by ⅜in, and you can cut these next. Those at the top are double-stopped, but the ends should not be finished until after final assembly. Round over the top edges as required. You can then clean up and glasspaper all inner edges of the side frames prior to assembling.

Because of the greasy nature of teak which sometimes prevents glue adhering properly, try brushing all the joints with methylated spirits before applying the glue; you must allow the spirits to dry off first but this only takes a few minutes. Allow the frames to remain in cramps overnight.

The next stage is to mark out the joints on the top end rails. While there is a conventional double tenon arrangement on the rails, you cannot mark out the mortises with a gauge because they are not parallel with the edges. You will have to use a rule and pencil, so be sure to check before cutting.

Follow on by cutting the eight mortises. While it is not normal practice to cut mortises when halfway through assembling, you will have to do so now

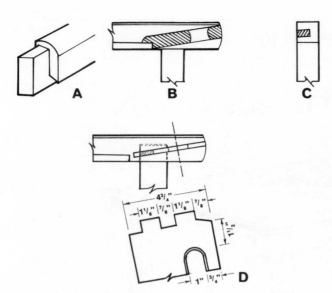

Fig. 30.1. (A), end of side rail; (B) section of handle. (C) shows how the top rail is mortise and tenoned to the leg – the shaded portion is then cut away to form a mortise for the tenon on the end rail, (D) details of end rail joints.

because of the coincidence of the side mortises with the leg tenons. If all the mortises were cut before assembling, the mortise for the leg would need a temporary plug on the inside when cutting the side mortise, and in any case the mortise would need trimming after assembling to cut away the tenon which obstructed the side rail.

Only when these top joints have been finished should you clean up and glasspaper the surfaces of the side frames and the lower cross rails. Another job is to finish the ends of the top rails to the curve shown in the illustrations.

Mark out the finger slot which creates the handle next, using a gauge to determine its extent. Bore 1in dia holes at the ends, and use a coping saw to cut out the waste. Generally you will find that shaped work of this kind is best done in two stages, the first being to get the required profile with the edges square, then to do the rounding over – to combine the two operations usually leads to the work being rather irregular. There are no short cuts to rounding the edges of an internal hole like this one; you will need to undertake some careful freehand work with a

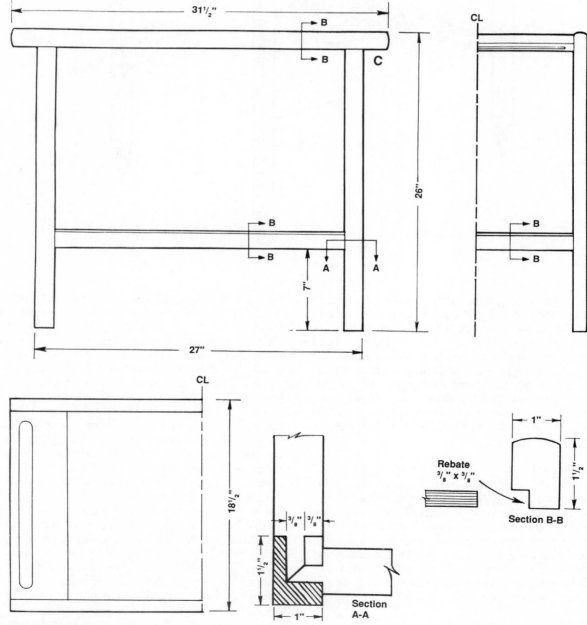

Fig. 30.2. Elevations and plan, with sections.

chisel, followed by glasspapering vigorously with a coarse grade at first to attain the required shape, and then finer grades to get a good finish.

The rebates on these end rails are not as straight-forward as the others, because of the slope of the rail. Probably the simplest way to work them is to cut them square initially, rather undersize, and then finish off with a shoulder plane so that they correspond with the sectional drawing shown. Notice that the lower edge of this rail is splayed slightly, both for improved appearance and for easier cleaning. You can clean up this rail all round except for the outer edge, this being attended to after assembly.

ASSEMBLY

Assemble the two side frames first and leave them cramped up for several hours. If you think it will strengthen the joints you can insert screws into the underside of the projecting top rail so that they pass through the outer of the double tenons.

Two items require completion at this stage. The ends of the stopped rebates will need a little attention to square off the corners, and the outer edge of the top rail has to be planed so that it is rounded over in line with the curved ends of the top side rails.

MAKING THE TRAYS

These were made from 6mm ply, faced on both sides with plastic laminate; you can either apply the laminate yourself or buy a piece ready–faced. If you do the job place the trays, when dealt with, between chip-board panels of similar size and put the whole thing into a small press to apply overall pressure; this should prevent any future distortion.

In either case you will need to trim and fit the trays to the rebates, fixing them with screws at approximately 4in centres.

FINISH

This is a matter of your choice but obviously the job will require a finish that will withstand a fair amount of wear and tear; a good quality polyester lacquer is probably the best.

Finally, a set of castors is required. Remember that for something like a dinner wagon which is very much a mobile piece of furniture, small castors are unsatisfactory, and you should choose the type which are sprung and with wheels of at least 3in dia.

CUTTING LIST

	INCHES			MM		
	L	W	T	L	W	T
4 legs	26¼	1¾	1	667	45	1
2 top side rails	32¼	1¾	1	819	45	25
2 top end rails	19	5	¾	482	127	19
2 bottom side rails	26¾	1¾	1	679	45	25
2 bottom end rails	19	1¾	1	482	45	25
1 top tray, ply	23¼	17½	¼	591	445	6
1 bottom tray, ply	25½	17½	¼	648	445	6
2 plastic laminates for top	23¼	17½	–	591	445	–
2 plastic laminates for bottom	25¼	17½	–	641	445	–

Working allowances have been made to lengths and widths; thicknesses are net.

SIDEBOARD WITH MIRROR-LINED COCKTAIL CABINET

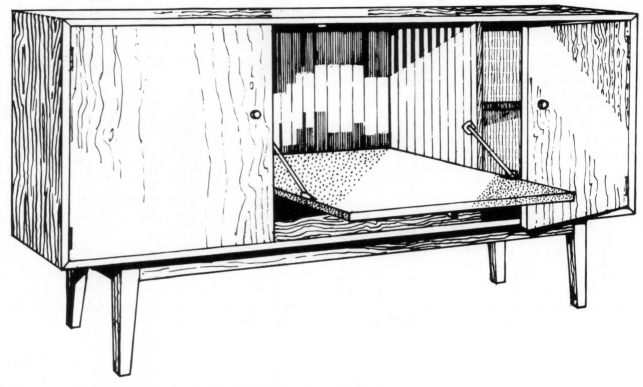

Fig. 31.1. The sideboard with the fall-flap down revealing the drinks compartment.

The carcase of this design, consisting of the top, the two ends, and the bottom, was made from solid timber – most mahogany types would be suitable – while the doors and the drop flap were made from laminboard or blockboard, lipped where required.

MAKING UP THE CARCASE

If you are using solid wood, you may need to joint up several boards to make up the necessary width. When you have done this, clean the work up and cut it to the exact lengths and widths shown in the drawings, working a rebate on the back edges for the ply back. Use mitred dovetails for the corners both at top and bottom; any other method is impracticable because of the moulded chamfered front. In setting out the dovetails, remember that the first dovetail pin has to be set ⅛in back from the chamfered edge.

The partitions D and the shelf E are fixed with stopped dovetail housing joints. Since the doors cover and finish flush with the edge of the partitions, make sure that the front edge of the latter is ¹³⁄₁₆in back from the chamfered edge. After cutting the joints, it's a convenient time to work the chamfered moulding.

Glue up the carcase and the two partitions and clean up the assembly, but do not glue in shelf E, as

this should be left until the drop front is ready for hingeing. Plane the ply back to fit in the rebate and screw it in place.

THE STOOL

Plane up the legs and rails to the correct width and thickness, and run the groove to accept the buttons in the rails. Taper the legs as shown and cut the mortises and tenons for the front, back, and end rails; these are ordinary haunched tenons, the rails finishing flush with the face of the legs. Glue and clean up, and fix the mid-rails with stopped dovetail housings, so that they centre on the partitions. Cut the stool legs and fix them to the carcase with wooden buttons.

DOORS AND DROP FLAP

As already mentioned, these are made from ¾in lamin- or blockboard, lipped as shown and veneered on both sides. Check that the veneer is horizontal, as the face veneer must be at right angles to that of the surface. Work tongues on the lippings as shown in Fig. 31.6, mitre their corners and glue them into the grooves – leave the lipping about ¹⁄₃₂in proud at each side of the door so that you can clean up flush with the laminboard.

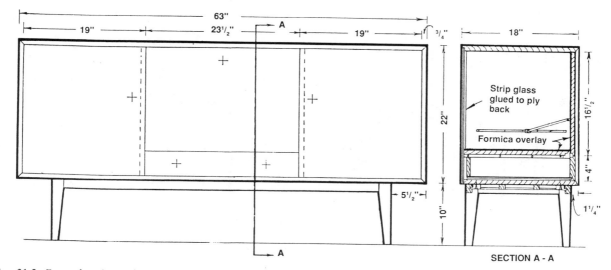

Fig. 31.2. Front elevation and section through end. Principal sizes are shown, although they can be varied to suit your requirements.

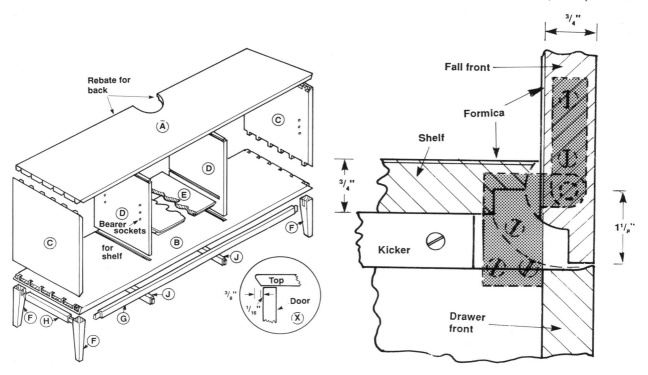

Fig. 31.3. How the parts are assembled.

Fig. 31.4. Section through hingeing edge of the fall-flap.

Plane the doors and the fall front about 1/16in larger than the finished size and veneer both sides. You can use either veneers that are the same as those on the carcase or contrasting ones, but in either case it is unlikely that a full width will be obtainable, so be careful to keep the joint dead central in each case. If you do choose a contrasting veneer, the door lippings should be the same material as the veneer.

Next, hang the doors, using 2in brass hinges, keeping the opening edge flush with the inner partition and allowing a 1/16in break from the chamfered edge.

FALL FRONT
This has been designed so that when open it is level with the shelf, and glasses and bottles can be pulled forward without the inconvenience of a step. The drawer is placed underneath, so that the shelf is at a convenient height (16in from the ground) for distributing and pouring drinks; this makes it necessary to

swing the front on a pin hinge and slightly curve the drawer front to allow clearance; and Fig. 31.4 shows the detail of this arrangement.

As the hinge has to be central to shelf E, you cannot use an ordinary straight pin hinge and you will need a cranked one. Such hinges may be difficult to obtain, but they are fairly simple to make from 1/8in thick brass sheet to the measurements given in Fig. 31.5. The pins are made from 1/4in dia brass rod, and the back of the cranked part is countersunk, and the pin riveted and filed off flush. Recess the hinges in flush with the partitions, with the centre of the pin in line with the centre line of the shelf.

Note that the depth of the fall front must be 1 1/8in larger than the centre of shelf E, and the greater this overlap is, the less curvature is necessary on the drawer and shelf front, but no useful purpose will be served by making it greater than 1 1/8in.

Plane the front to fit between the doors, allowing enough clearance for it to swing freely. Check half

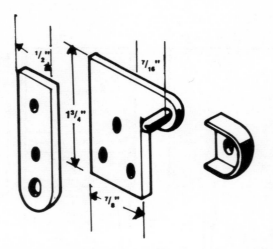

Fig. 31.5. Details of the special hinges.

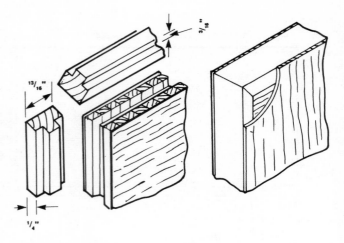

Fig. 31.6. Details of the door lipping.

the bottom as shown and round the inside edge. Screw in one cranked hinge, fix the socket to it, locate the other crank of the other hinge in the opposite socket, and screw it in place. The front of the cranked part of the hinge prevents the doors from closing fully, so you will have to chisel a notch out of the door edges to allow them to shut.

You can improve the appearance by either making a brass shoe to insert as in Fig. 31.5, or by gluing a piece of ebony or plastic into the door edge and chiselling it to fit the hinge projection. Ensure that there is ample clearance in both cases, as the object is to present a good appearance when the door is open rather than to make a close joint. You may find some adjustment is necessary to get the front and doors exactly flush, but take care to get them correct as an uneven frontage looks bad.

Next, you can slide the shelf E into position, and after checking the front and hollowing it to fit the fall front, mark off the depth and plane to size; you can now glue it in place and cramp the assembly up.

COCKTAIL CABINET

You can finish the interior of this in two ways, either with a light coloured veneer such as sycamore, or with a good quality plastic laminate. The latter is certainly more durable as it is impervious to most stains and can be wiped over easily; although sycamore and other veneers that are light in colour look attractive when new, they are liable to discolour with age and use even though you have treated them with a modern synthetic lacquer. But before you start this stage of the work, read the paragraph dealing with fitting mirror strips.

The last job on this section is to chamfer the external edges of the fall and sides so that they close snugly, and this can be done with a bullnose plane.

THE DRAWER

The usual method of drawer construction is used, but note that the sides are slightly lower than the front, which is hollowed to allow the fall front to open.

Fit and screw a kicker to the partitions under the shelf E to prevent the drawer tilting on being opened. Veneer the drawer front on both sides – it might be possible to manage with a front veneer only as the drawer is shallow, but to be on the safe side it is better to veneer both front and back. Don't forget

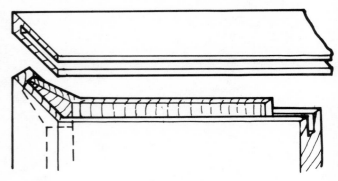

Fig. 31.7. How the loose shelves are clamped.

that the joint of the veneer on the drawer front should coincide with the veneer joint on the fall front. Glue two small stops to the bottom of the carcase so that they butt against the back of the drawer front and thus ensure that the drawer finishes flush with the doors and the fall.

FITTING UP

Mirror strips make a suitably glamorous finish for the back of the cocktail cupboard and can be bought at any good hardware store; the material is made of strips of thin mirror glass, glued to a fabric backing. To fix it, carefully draw round the inside of the cupboard on to the ply back, remove it, and fix the mirror backing with a contact adhesive. This job should be done before you fix the plastic laminate sides and bottom so they can then finish close to the mirror strips and give a neat, close joint.

The doors and fall front are held in place with magnetic catches, one for each door and two for the fall front. The front is supported by stays and they should be fairly large with, say, a 9in to 10in arm; if they are made of nylon they will be noiseless and practically everlasting. Choose some unobtrusive handles to suit this design – those used in the original were ¾in dia brass ones.

You can make the two loose shelves from either laminated board in the same manner as the doors, or from solid wood clamped on both ends and the front as shown in Fig. 31.6. The supports for these shelves can be placed at any convenient heights, but a central shelf with one at 2in above and below is generally satisfactory.

If the drawer is to be used for cutlery, try fitting a loose tray divided into compartments rather than dividing the drawer itself; no tray is illustrated as obviously its design depends on individual requirements.

CUTTING LIST

		INCHES			MM	
Part	L	W	T	L	W	T
A 1 top	63½	18¼	¾	1612	464	19
B 1 bottom	63½	18¼	¾	1612	464	19
C 2 ends	22½	18¼	¾	572	464	19
D 2 partitions	22	17¼	¾	559	438	19
E 1 shelf	24½	17¼	¾	622	438	19
1 back, ply	63	20	3/16	1600	508	5
2 doors	19½	21	¾	495	533	19
1 drop-front	17	24	¾	432	610	19
1 drawer front	24	4¼	¾	610	108	19
1 drawer back	24	3½	½	610	89	13
2 drawer sides	17½	4½	½	445	108	13
2 drawer runners	17½	¾	½	445	19	13

CUTTING LIST (continued)

		INCHES			MM	
	L	W	T	L	W	T
1 drawer bottom, ply	24	17¼	3/16	610	438	5
2 loose shelves	16	16	⅝	407	407	16
2 front clamps for shelves	19	1¾	⅝	482	45	16
4 side clamps for shelves	17½	1¾	⅝	445	45	16
4 door lippings	22	⅞	½	559	22	13
4 door lippings	19	⅞	½	483	22	13
2 drop-front lippings	24	⅞	½	610	22	13
2 drop-front lippings	17	⅞	½	432	22	13
F 4 stool legs	10½	2	1¾	267	51	45
G 2 stool rails	53	1⅝	⅞	1346	42	22
H 2 stool rails	16½	1⅝	⅞	419	42	22
J 2 mid-rails	16½	1⅝	⅞	419	42	22

Working allowances have been made to lengths and widths; thicknesses are net.

AN ELEGANT SIDEBOARD WITH MAXIMUM STORAGE

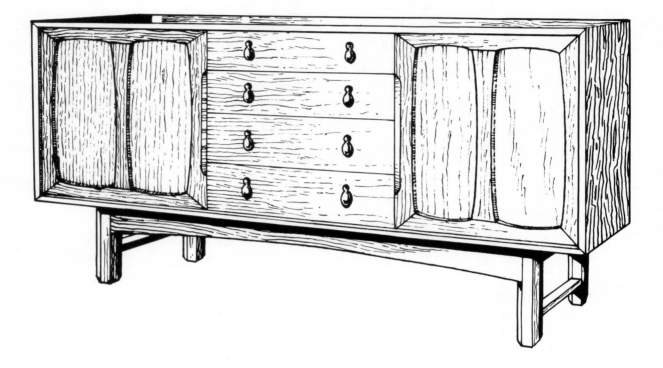

The design had to hold the contents of a small chest of drawers, a bureau, and a sewing box; also it had to contain a number of drawers of varying depths, and about four shelves. In other words it had to hold quite a variety of different things and, of course, look good at the same time.

Afrormosia-veneered blockboard was used in the carcase, and solid afrormosia for the lippings, the door frames, and the underframe. The door panels were in American black walnut-veneered plywood, and this was also laminated to the main drawer fronts. The finish was in a matt polyurethane lacquer, and the handles were satin finished aluminium.

CONSTRUCTION

To get the maximum out of the afrormosia block-board, cut three lengths each 15¾in wide; these will cut the top, bottom, ends, and divisions; all you will then need are the two cupboard shelves.

Work rebates on the top, bottom, and sides ⅜in by ½in to take the ¼in ply back, and you will also have to groove them ⅜in deep by ¼in to take the lippings. Screw and glue the top and bottom to the sides as shown in Fig. 32.2, and finish them at the corners with a ¾in by ¾in afrormosia corner bead; glue and cramp this on to set overnight.

Now you can fix the ¼in ply back, making sure it is cut square so that the carcase will accept it. The lippings to the carcase are 2½in by ¾in afrormosia, bevelled at 45 degrees; groove them to take the track for the doors to slide on. Complete this stage by

cleaning off and glasspapering the corner beads and edgings.

Assuming you have lipped the divisions with the afrormosia and cleaned them up, you can fix them next. They are grooved at the top to take a ¼in by ¼in hardwood strip which you should glue and screw to the underside of the top first. Remember to allow a slightly greater distance between the two divisions to allow the door clearance for the drawer behind it to open. Glue the division and slide it into the ¼in by ¼in strip glued and screwed from under-neath; see Fig. 32.3.

Finally, when you have bevelled and cleaned off the shelves you can fix them in exactly the same way as the division in Fig. 32.3, by screwing through the division and grooving it into a ¼in by ¼in strip which you have glued and screwed to the end of the unit. Once this has been done, inspect the carcase for any damage or scratches which you should make good now as they always show up more once the piece has been polished.

THE DRAWERS

The next step is to make and fit the two drawers situated at the top of each cupboard; they are only 3in deep but it is surprising what they hold! One drawer is divided into compartments for sewing and knitting requisites, and the other for stationery etc. The sides are out of ½in beech, the divisions are ¼in, and the front 3in by ¾in walnut bevelled to form a hand grip as shown in Fig. 32.4. The front and back

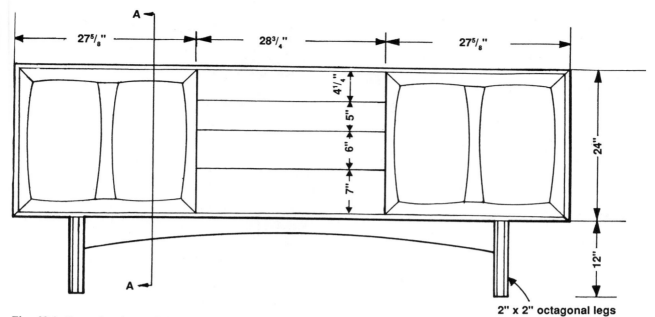

Fig. 32.1. Front elevation with dimensions.

corners are dovetailed and the 3/16in ply bottom is grooved into the sides and fronts; the drawer runs on two hardwood runners screwed and glued to the sides.

Make the four central drawers from plywood, with 1/2in thick fronts and sides, and 1/4in thick bottoms; glue the 1/4in American black walnut ply to the drawer fronts and veneer the top edges with a matching veneer. You will have to groove each drawer side to accept a hardwood runner which is 3/16in wide by 5/16in thick. You can glue and pin the drawer parts together, the bottoms being grooved into the fronts and sides.

THE DOORS
These have mitred and keyed frames, which is a little unusual and quite effective.

The surround frame is 2in by 3/4in and the centre rail is 3in by 3/4in; Use 3/8in thick plywood dovetail keys to joint the mitres from the back; the keys are blind – in other words they do not penetrate through to the front – and you can glue and screw them in place as in Fig. 32.5. I made a template of the bottom rail and one of the stile to make sure I got the keys all the same.

You can cut the rails to the exact length, and then rebate them 7/8in by 1/2in; it is a large rebate to allow for subsequent shaping. Also groove the bottom rail 1/4in by 1/4in so that it will slide on the afrormosia runner.

Once this is done use the templates mentioned above to mark the door frame rails and stiles and cut them to shape with either a jigsaw or a bowsaw and finish with glasspaper. Now you have to cut the handles into the stiles as in Fig. 32.6, and if you

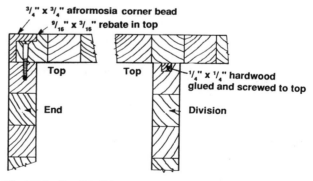

Fig. 32.3. Details of the top.

Fig. 32.2. Section A–A from Fig 1.

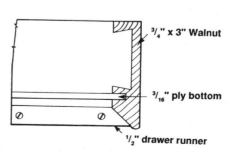

Fig. 32.4. Drawer section.

111

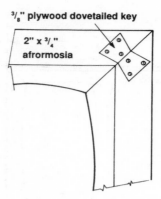

Fig. 32.5. Showing the dovetail key in the door corner.

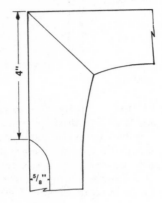

Fig. 32.6. Details of mitering and chamfering.

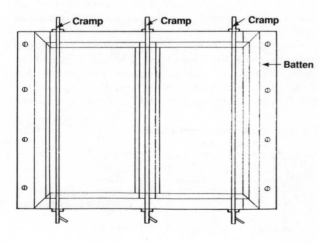

Fig. 32.7. Jig for cramping up the doors.

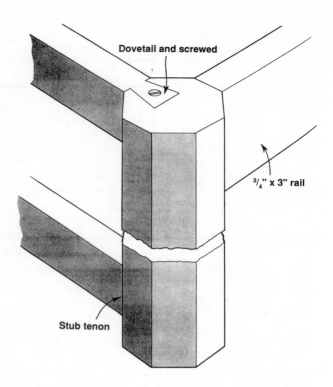

Fig. 32.8. Detail of dovetail fixing into leg.

THE UNDERFRAMING

This is in solid afrormosia, the legs being 2in by 2in, octagonal, with the front and back rails 3in by ¾in thick. You can see the method of construction from Fig. 32.8 and it is relatively straightforward. Remember to groove the front and back rails to receive eight hardwood buttons, although you can pocket-screw directly up through the side rails as an alternative.

Assemble the two small frames first, making sure they are square; you can then glue and fix the two long rails.

FINISH

As already mentioned, the finish was matt polyurethane lacquer. Having thoroughly cleaned off and glasspapered the whole job, wipe it over with a tack rag to collect any remaining dust. Apply the polyurethane lacquer in accordance with the manufacturer's instructions and allow it a day to dry. Give the job three coats, glasspapering each one lightly to remove any nibs. After the final coat has dried hard, use fine wire wool impregnated with wax polish – this will dull the shine and give a matt satin finish. If, however, you want a gloss finish, give the job another coat and glasspaper it lightly with flour paper. Then apply wax polish with a muslin cloth, and burnish it up with a soft lint-free duster.

possess a circular saw it is a simple operation to set two stops and 'drop the stile on'; otherwise you can get the same effect with chisels, rasps, and glasspaper but it will take a little longer.

Cramping up the doors is easier if you make a jig, (Fig. 32.7), which is a piece of chipboard with two battens screwed on as shown; make sure that the size between the battens is the same width as the doors. Fit the ¼in ply panels dry and fix them with beads screwed into the rebate; then stub-tenon the centre muntins into the top and bottom rails. Finally, glue the mitres and keys into place and cramp the assemblies up and leave them for the glue to set. Two flush bolts are fitted to each door.

CUTTING LIST

	INCHES			MM		
	L	W	T	L	W	T
Carcase						
1 top	83⅝	15¾	¾	2124	400	19
1 bottom	83⅝	15¾	¾	2124	400	19
2 ends	22½	15¾	¾	571	400	19
2 divisions	22½	13¾	¾	571	349	19
2 shelves	28	11¼	¾	711	285	19
2 lippings	87	2½	¾	2210	64	19
2 lippings	27	2½	¾	686	64	19
2 lippings	28	2½	¾	711	64	19
2 lippings	27	1¼	¾	686	32	19
4 corner beadings	21	1	¾	533	25	19
1 door runner	84	½	¼	2133	13	6
1 back	83½	23½	¼	2121	597	6
4 loose tongues	16	½	¼	406	13	6
Interior drawers						
2 fronts	28	3	¾	711	76	19
2 backs	28	2½	½	711	64	13
4 sides	16	2½	½	406	64	13
2 bottoms, ply	28	16	3⁄16	711	406	5
4 runners	16	¾	½	406	19	13
Doors						
4 top & bottom rails	28	2	¾	711	51	19
4 stiles	24	2	¾	609	51	19
2 muntins	24	3	¾	609	76	19
8 beadings	24	½	¼	609	13	6
8 beadings	12	½	¼	305	13	6
4 panels	24	12	¼	609	305	6

CUTTING LIST (continued)

	INCHES			MM		
	L	W	T	L	W	T
Centre drawers						
1 front	29	7	½	737	178	13
1 front	29	6	½	737	153	13
1 front	29	5	½	737	127	13
1 front	29	4¼	½	737	108	13
1 back	29	6½	½	737	165	13
1 back	29	5½	½	737	140	13
1 back	29	4½	½	737	115	13
1 back	29	3¾	½	737	95	13
2 sides	16	7	½	406	178	13
2 sides	16	6	½	406	153	13
2 sides	16	5	½	406	127	13
2 sides	16	4¼	½	406	108	13
4 bottoms	29	16	¼	737	406	6
1 front facing	29	7	¼	737	178	6
1 front facing	29	6	¼	737	153	6
1 front facing	29	5	¼	737	127	6
1 front facing	29	4¼	¼	737	108	6
8 slips	16	¾	5⁄16	406	19	8
4 veneers	29	⅞	–	737	22	–
Stool underframe						
4 legs	13	2¼	2	330	57	51
2 long rails	66	3	¾	1676	76	19
2 end rails	15	1¼	1	381	32	25
8 buttons	2	1	¾	51	25	19

Working allowances have been made to lengths and widths; thicknesses are net.

CIRCULAR DINING TABLE

This four foot diameter circular dining table was made with 1in thick blockboard which was veneered with rosewood and lipped around the edge with 1in solid rosewood. The legs and cross rails were made of prime seasoned and selected joinery softwood.

GENERAL REMARKS

The top frame comprises four thicknesses of best quality hardboard glued together and cramped up until set in a former; however, you could use ⅛in thick plywood if you prefer.

The frame structure has a flat painted eggshell finish which is first primed and then filled and lightly rubbed down. Several coats of clear (white) French polish can be applied with a pad to the table top to give an elegant finish, and you can impart a matt surface by allowing each coat to set hard and then rubbing the grain with fine steel wool impregnated with wax. In the design illustrated the frame is painted softwood, but of course you could use a hardwood if you require a polished finish.

MAKING THE FORMER FOR THE FRAME

You will need a baseboard 48in by 18in and at least ¾in thick; or you could use the flat working surface of your bench if it is large enough.

Mark out the baseboard as shown in Fig. 8 with a vertical centre line, then fixing the baseboard to the floor and extending the centre line. If you have a beam compass, set it to 21½in radius and describe the perimeter arc. If you don't have such an instrument, you can improvise a substitute with a long thin strip of wood, one end of which you notch to take a pencil; tap a pin through the strip to give you the appropriate radius and you have your beam compass.

Mark a right angle equally about the centre line approximately 4in down from the top edge; blocks (A) and (I) are located 45 degrees each side of the centre line. The right angle is divided up equally into eight sectors, each being 11 degrees 15 minutes.

Make the nine blocks each 4in high, 1½in wide, and 3in thick, with all corners squared off. Glue and screw them from the underside of the board, and set each one centrally at a sector junction on the perimeter arc. Mark a centre line on each lamination, the length of which is approximately 36in at this stage, and align this line with the centre line at the block (E), which is clamped first; subsequently, blocks (C), (G), (A), and (I) are all aligned in the same way.

When you have made up all four sectors, prepare and clean up the laminations to 4in wide; the length around the outside perimeter of each section is 34⁴⁄₇in (a trifle over 34½in). Finally, mark out and cut the shouldered tenons as shown in Fig. 5, and also work the ¼in grooves for the fastening buttons.

You will need to interpose a plastic sheet or

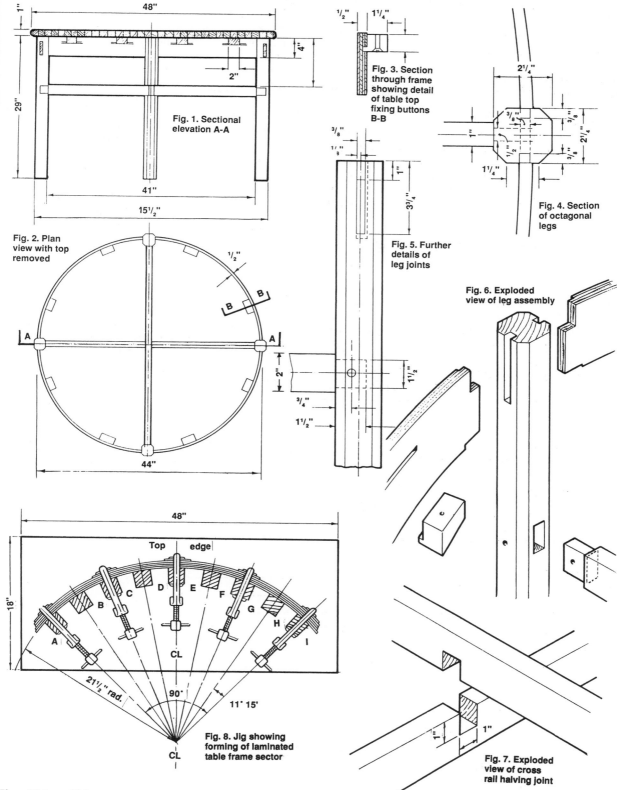

Fig. 1. Sectional elevation A-A

Fig. 2. Plan view with top removed

Fig. 3. Section through frame showing detail of table top fixing buttons B-B

Fig. 4. Section of octagonal legs

Fig. 5. Further details of leg joints

Fig. 6. Exploded view of leg assembly

Fig. 7. Exploded view of cross rail halving joint

Fig. 8. Jig showing forming of laminated table frame sector

Figs. 33.1. to 33.8.

newspaper between the former and the laminations to stop them sticking to each other.

LEGS

The four legs are octagonally shaped and parallel throughout their length. First of all cut them to length and prepare them as 2¼in squares. Mark diagonal centre lines at each end from each adjoining face, and complete the octagonal ends as in Fig. 4. After planing each leg to shape, mark and prepare the top through shouldered mortises for each corres-

ponding tenon on the frame sector ends; identifying each joint assembly will greatly assist during gluing up.

CROSS RAILS

Prepare these to finish 2in by 1in and cut them to a 44in length. Cut the shouldered tenons at each end and mark them with a distinguishing mark. Then work the stopped mortise joints in the legs for these rails on the inner face of each leg as shown in Figs. 4 and 5, and cut the notched halving joint at the central right angle intersection of the rails as detailed in Fig. 7.

Finish this stage by glasspapering all parts to a smooth finish ready for assembly.

ORDER OF ASSEMBLY

Glue and lightly cramp up the two cross rails at the halving joint. Then glue and cramp up the assembled cross rails into each leg, holding them until the glue has set by sash cramps applied across each opposite pair of legs. Check that each leg is perfectly upright from all directions.

You can drill this joint (where the cross rail intersects the leg) for a ³⁄₈in dowel which is glued in place; now leave this part-assembly to dry without further disturbance.

The next stage is to glue the frame sectors into their relative positions with the assembly upside down – this makes sure that the frame top surfaces finish flat and in line for the final positioning of the top without any distortion.

Fit a 'Spanish windlass' or a band cramp around the assembled frame into the legs. You can make a Spanish windlass from strong string or nylon cord, inserting protective pads where it crosses the outer face of the legs, and threading a length of dowel through the string and twisting it like a tourniquet to pull each frame sector fully into the leg joint. When it is removed, you can prime and finish painting the completed table frame.

THE TABLE TOP

Use your beam compass to mark this out on the underside to 47¾in diameter. It is a good idea, at the same time, to describe a 44in diameter line (also on the underside) to help you to position the top frame correctly. This band on the underside should also be painted completely before finally fixing the top.

Although you could use a bowsaw for the next task of cutting out the top, a bandsaw will make a much better job as it will automatically produce the square edge that is essential for fixing the lipped edge neatly.

Next make the eight buttons which hold the top

as shown in Figs. 1 and 3; drill and countersink them for 1⁷⁄₈in by 8 screws. Now locate the top carefully on to the frame, and screw the buttons into position with their tongues in the grooves you cut earlier. Don't use glue when fixing them as their function is to allow shrinking to take place without any splitting occurring.

The lippings can be prepared now; you will need two, each being 1in wide by ⅛in thick. Pencil a centre line across the top to match up with the centre line of two opposite legs; you can then cut each strip to length and bend it round for a dry fit.

As each strip requires a number of cramps (at least six), glue one strip first and cramp it up, using protective pads of hardboard or thin ply between the cramps and the wood. Allow the glue to set before removing the cramps ready for fixing the second strip in the same manner. You can tap in a 1in panel pin at an angle at the ends of each strip for additional holding, punching their heads below the surface and filling them. As a last resort if you do not have enough cramps, you could fix the lipping in four equal pieces.

Finally work a ⅛in radius on the top and bottom edges of the lippings. The top is now ready for you to go over it with a cabinet scraper, followed by the usual sequence of glasspapering to produce a flawless top surface.

CUTTING LIST

	INCHES			MM		
	L	W	T	L	W	T
1 top	48	4	1	1219	102	25
4 legs	29½	2½	2¼	749	64	58
2 cross rails	44½	2¼	1	1130	58	25
16 frame laminations	35½	4¼	⅛	902	108	3
8 top buttons, from						
1 piece	12	2¼	1⅛	305	58	29
2 lippings	76	1¼	⅛	1930	32	3

Working allowances have been made to lengths and widths; thicknesses are net.

Two Tables From One Basic Design

I used Kara redwood (a Russian softwood) for these, and first prepared a full-sized drawing of the table frame (Fig. 34.1) so I could make up the caul for the rails. I found that the finished rail sprang about ¼in at each end, so the curve of the caul needed to be tightened by this amount to allow for it.

MAKING THE CAUL
I made this from secondhand joists, 2in thick, glued and screwed together. Although it had to be precise and square, the inside and outside curves had different radii which called for two bandsaw cuts; the difference was of course the thickness of the rail. I cleaned up the caul with a spokeshave and a compass plane to exact dimensions.

THE LAMINATED RAILS
These came next and they were all of redwood. Each quarter of the table needed nine laminations 3mm thick; all of them were keyed with a toothing plane, except for the facing laminations which only needed toothing on one side.

I used Aerolite 306 adhesive to make up the rails, and as a quantity was needed I stored it in a screw-topped glass jar – if it is kept airtight it does not set for several days. I found the easiest way to glue up the rails was to take a set of laminations and apply the hardener to both sides of four pieces and adhesive to the other surfaces. I interleaved these layers so that

the hardener and the adhesive came together, after which I placed the assembly into the caul, interposing a layer of cartridge paper between the surface of the caul and the assembly in case any adhesive was transferred. Sash cramps applied the necessary pressure, and the assembly was left in the caul for 24 hours to set. I had to repeat this process four times to make all the rails.

Using nine 3mm layers gave enough thickness for cleaning up the spots where the rail was marked by the edge of the caul. I found the best way of cleaning the edges was to put each of the rails back into the caul, plane one edge straight and square to the surface of the caul, gauge it to the correct width (4in) and plane it down to the line.

THE LEGS
Next I planed up the legs from 3in by 2in stuff. They were surfaced and thicknessed to 1¾in and I made a hardboard template for the shape of the legs which splay out at the ends and curve throughout their length to give a nice balance to the table. I used the template to mark out the legs although the joints were cut before the legs were shaped.

By doing it this way I could mark out the joints from the square edge. The joints were double twin mortises and tenons cut right through the legs from both sides, giving a ⅞in long tenon on each of the rails (Fig. 34.2). I set out the joints using two gauges

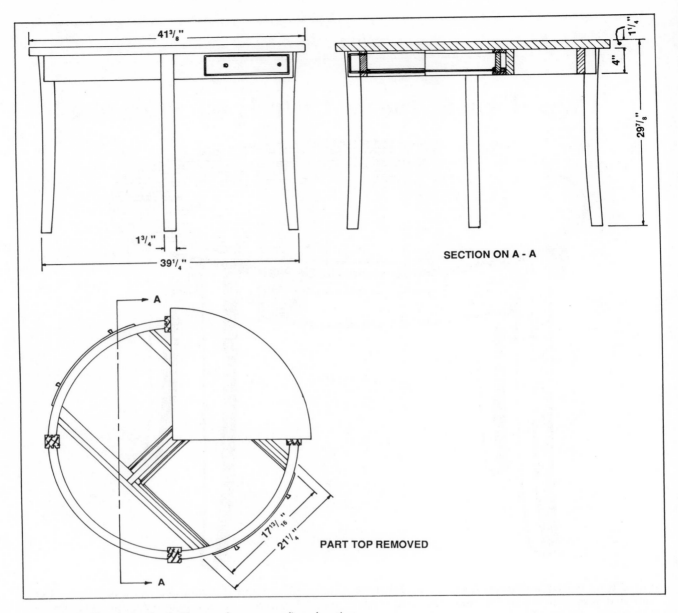

Fig. 34.1. Elevations, plan (with part of top removed), and section.

and to obtain a good accurate position for them I cramped a block to the inside of the rails and set the gauges from this. These angles are critical and were taken very carefully from the drawing.

By making twin tenons a centre portion is left for strength and the haunch at the top gives more stability at the top of the rail. Once the joints were cut I cramped them up to check that all the shoulders fitted accurately – I used a flexible bandcramp for this as well as for the final gluing up.

TABLE FITTED WITH DRAWERS

Having completed the frame I had to decide whether the table was to be fitted with drawers or an extending leaf because, of course, the construction differs.

For the table which was fitted with a pair of drawers, the drawer support rails had to be positioned and the mortises cut into the front and back rails (Fig 34.3); these rails were 4in by ¾in thick and were positioned centrally and 19¾in apart. I worked twin mortise and tenon joints to hold them in place and jointed a centre rail in the same way to tie the rails together and hold them parallel throughout their length.

Then I marked out the drawer fronts on the two

opposite rails. The fronts are 3⅛in by 17¾in long (the last measurement is a straight length, not one round the curve). I drilled a hole just large enough to accept a coping saw blade in the corner of the drawer front and sawed out the front. It was necessary to start the cuts with a coping saw but as much as possible was cut with a tenon saw to ensure that the cut was straight.

Having removed the front, I squared up the sides of the hole with a large chisel and then planed the drawer front square as well. The front is therefore smaller than the space it was cut from by about ⁵⁄₁₆in and I made a simple moulding and planted it on all the edges of the front. The moulding was allowed to project ⅛in on the face of the drawer (Fig. 34.4), and once the moulding was glued in place the front could be fitted into the drawer opening.

The kickers and runners were glued and screwed on the inside of the drawer support rails and I took care that these were parallel so that the drawer would run smoothly. Having done this, I fitted a fill-in piece on top of the runners as I had deliberately made the rails wider than the drawer front to make the jointing easier (Fig. 34.1).

This completed, the frame was cleaned up, sealed

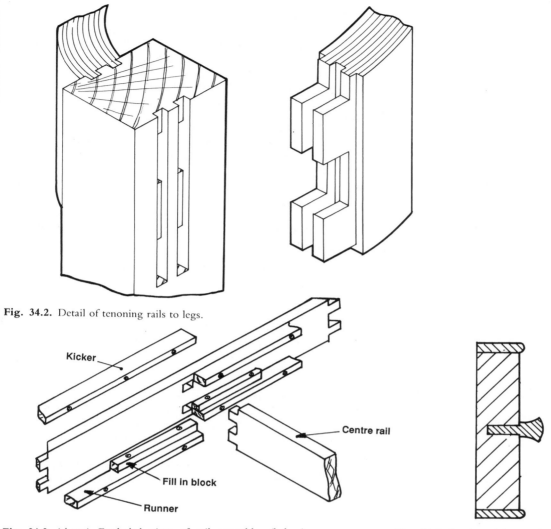

Fig. 34.2. Detail of tenoning rails to legs.

Kicker

Centre rail

Fill in block

Runner

Fig. 34.3. (above) Exploded view of rail assembly: (below) framing detail.

Fig. 34.4. Section of drawer front and knob.

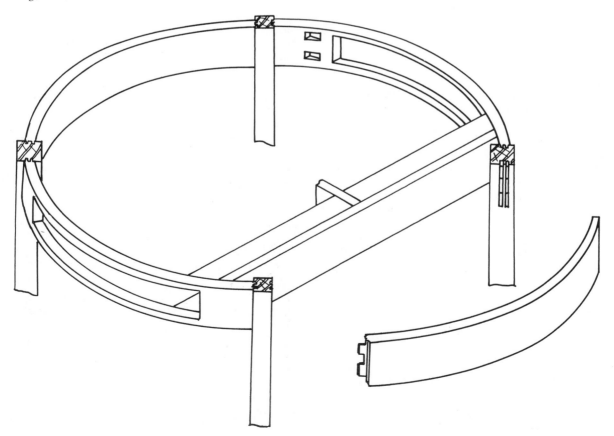

119

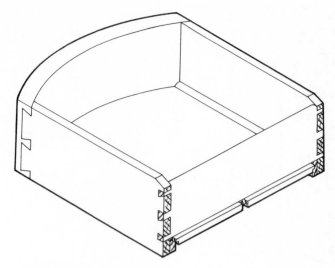

Fig. 34.5. Drawer construction.

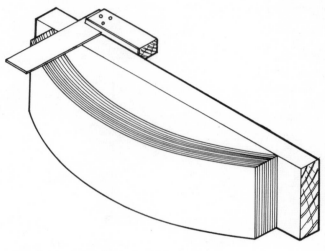

Fig. 34.6. Marking out drawer front.

with polyurethane varnish diluted 10% with white spirit, and then glued up.

DRAWER CONSTRUCTION
This is shown in Fig. 34.5 and is the traditional method of construction. I lap-dovetailed the front corner joints, having first cut through the moulding which was on the face of the end of the drawer front.

As the fronts were bowed there were problems in making the drawer, and to overcome them I planed the timber to the size and the thickness of the sides, gauged to the inside of the drawer fronts. I placed a board across the back edge of the front and used a try square off this board, (Fig. 34.6).

Then I cut and fitted the joints as shown in Fig. 34.5, followed by the back joints. The back was narrower than the sides because the drawer bottom ran under the bottom edge of the back; it could then be replaced quickly at any future time and also it was easier to fit.

Once the joints were fitted, I cut the groove into the inside of the front and also in the drawer slips. The upper edge of the back and the top edges of the drawer slips were rounded with a plane and glass-papered; the slips were then notched into the groove in the front.

I cleaned and glued up the drawers, cut the bottoms in 4mm plywood and fitted them into the slips.

By gently planing the edges of the slips I fitted the bottoms into the drawers and glued the slips in place; the back edge of each drawer bottom was held with a ⅝in brass screw. A gentle skim with a plane was enough to ensure that the drawers slid easily in the rails and for good measure a rub with candlewax acted as a lubricant.

MAKING THE TOP
This is made by rub-jointing several 1⅜in thick planks together, making sure that the direction of the heartwood of each one is opposed to that of its neighbour; after the glue had set I planed these flat and thicknessed them to finish 1¼in.

Next I marked out the circular top, using a piece of string and a centre pin as a pair of compasses, and then bandsawed it to size and planed the edge to a smooth contour with a compass plane.

To hold the top to the base I made a series of flat brass plates and let them into the top edge of the table rails, having elongated the screw holes to allow for possible shrinkage in the manner of slot-screwing.

I turned the handles for the drawers from red deal to the shape shown in Fig. 34.4 with ¼in round pins turned on the ends to fit into drilled holes in the fronts.

FINISH
Having completed the construction I cleaned up and glasspapered the job and softened the edges to a pencil finish. I applied three coats of polyurethane varnish with a brush, the first being diluted with 10% white spirit and the final coat an eggshell finish. I then flatted off the surface by rubbing it lightly with fine steel wool, followed by an application of wax polish.

EXTENDING TABLE
Everything in the construction of the extending table was the same, except that the drawer fronts were not cut out and there was no centre rail to support the side rails until the two rails for the centre leaf support had been fixed in place. These rails were fitted in the same way as the drawer support rails but spaced 18⅜in apart instead of 19¾in – this was because the centre leaf was 17¾in wide, and the extra ⅝in was to allow for the locating pegs in the table edges.

The centre leaf was made from three pieces rub-jointed and planed to the same thickness as the top. Having prepared the top and centre leaves, I cut the latter in half and fitted a pair of cylindrical hinges which allowed the top to fold in half without the hinges showing.

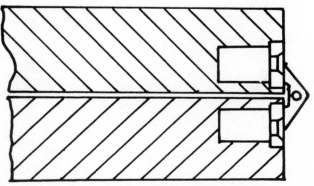

Fig. 34.7. Section of leaf (folded) showing cylindrical hinge fixing.

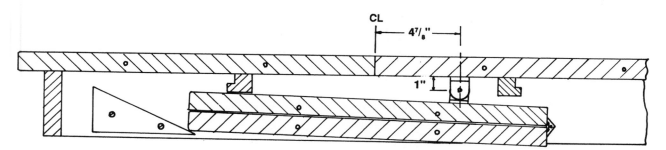

Fig. 34.8. Section through table showing the top in open and closed positions.

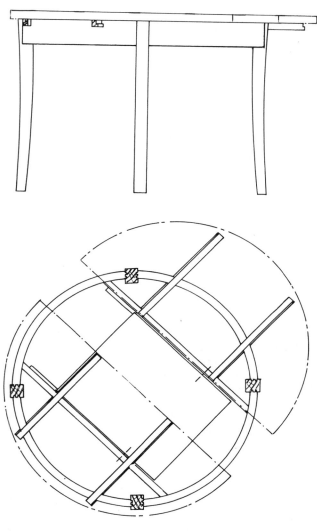

Fig. 34.9. Shows elevation and plan of the top in open and closed positions.

I had to gauge the centre of the hinge leaves while they were in position, and bored the holes to receive the body. Once this was fitted, I could mark out the leaf and cut the recess to take it. When the hinges had been positioned and fitted properly with the leaf folding over on itself, I pivoted the centre leaf from the support rails. To allow the leaf to fold and store in the centre of the table, the centre of this pivot was placed 4⅞in from the centre line and 1in from the top edge (Fig. 34.9). The pivots were made from folded brass strip with a steel pin silver-soldered in place to form the pivot; I made brass bushes to fit into 5/16in dia holes drilled in the rails, and then screwed two

tapered pieces of wood to the inside of the support rails for the leaf to slide on.

I made the top in two halves joined together with brass pins and bushes. Once these were fitted together I cut the circular top to shape and matched these pins and bushes to those on the centre leaf.

When the top was fitted, I made the lopers with a rebate on one edge so that they prevented the top dropping as it was extended. Next, I cut the slots in the guide rails and screwed the lopers to the underside of the top parallel to each other and square to the straight edge of the table top. So that the lopers gave enough support to the extended leaf I positioned them 14³⁄₁₆in apart; they were further supported by slots cut in both the circular side rails and the support rails.

CUTTING LIST

	INCHES			MM		
	L	W	T	L	W	T
1 top	42½	42	1¼	1078	1065	32
4 legs	29⅛	3	1¾	740	75	45
36 rail laminations	30¾	4	⅛	780	100	3
2 drawer supports	33¼	4	¾	845	100	19
1 centre rail	20¾	4	¾	530	100	19
4 runners	16½	1⅝	⅝	420	40	15
4 kickers	16½	1⅝	⅝	420	40	15
4 fill-in pieces	16½	1	¾	420	25	19
4 drawer sides	15¾	2¾	⅜	400	70	10
2 drawer backs	17¾	2¼	⅜	450	58	10
2 drawer bottoms, ply	17¾	17⅞	³⁄₁₆	450	455	5
4 drawer slips	15¾	⅝	⅜	400	16	10
1 piece for handles	7⅞	¾	⅝	200	19	16
1 moulding	83	3⅜	³⁄₁₆	2100	85	5

Alternative cutting list

1 top	42½	42	1¼	1078	1065	32
4 legs	29⅛	3	1¾	740	75	45
36 rail laminations	30¾	4	⅛	780	100	3
2 support rails	33⅛	4	¾	840	100	19
1 centre leaf	42	17¾	1¼	1065	450	32
4 lopers	18⅞	1¼	1	480	32	25
2 leaf slides	5⅞	2¾	⅜	150	70	10

Working allowances have been made to lengths and widths; thicknesses are net.

EXTENDING DINING TABLE

A feature of this table is the ingenious up-and-over action of the extension leaf made possible by using cylindrical hinges. When closed, four dining chairs will fit neatly underneath, forming a compact ensemble; extended, the table is large enough for eight people to dine in comfort. The design illustrated was made in mahogany with a sapele veneered top; the extension was cross-veneered in figured Rio rosewood, and the underframing was mahogany.

THE LEGS

The most convenient and quick method of turning the legs is to employ the 'profile board' technique. You need a pair of profile boards about 29in long, with a line gauged from the lower edge to indicate the centre line of the lathe and the leg. Shape the top edges of the boards to the half profile of the legs (see Fig. 35.2) and mark the mortise positions. Before removing each finished leg from the lathe, square the mortise size on to the leg and gauge the thickness. Check with a spirit level to make sure that the mortises intersect at right angles.

When you chop the mortises, try holding the legs in a vice with hollowed softwood pads on each side, and another beneath to provide a solid bed; this should make the job easier. Although some craftsmen may prefer it, a haunched joint is not really necessary; the hollowed end of the rail butting against the leg acts like a haunch to prevent possible movement.

RAILS

Prepare the side and end rails to 4¼in by 1in, and then mark the length and the tenon shoulders; you can gauge the extent of the narrower portion of the rails from the top edge. You can place a lath along this line and tap pins through it into the waste; it can then be bent to obtain a fair line for the curved bottom edge.

After you have sawn the tenons, you can cut the shoulders; cramp a bevelled block of wood to the leg to ensure that the saw is canted at the correct angle to make a good fit against the leg. You can either mitre or halve the ends of the tenons where they meet.

The mortises in the side rails that accept the centre rail stub-tenons can be chopped after you have first cut ⅛in deep stopped housings. Before assembly, round off the bottom edges of the rails slightly with a finely set spokeshave followed by glasspapering.

ASSEMBLY

The side rails and legs are assembled first and you will need hollowed softwood blocks under the sash cramps to protect the surfaces; you can then complete the frame assembly by gluing up the end and centre rails.

TABLE TOP

Before you cut the blockboard for the table top you will have to decide how it is to be veneered, bearing in mind that it is imperative for the grain of the blockboard veneer to run at right angles to the decorative veneer.

On the table illustrated, the lippings were glued but not tongued to the blockboard, thus making a

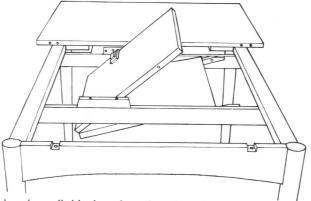

Fig. 35.1. One top removed and the other pulled back to show the action of the extending leaf.

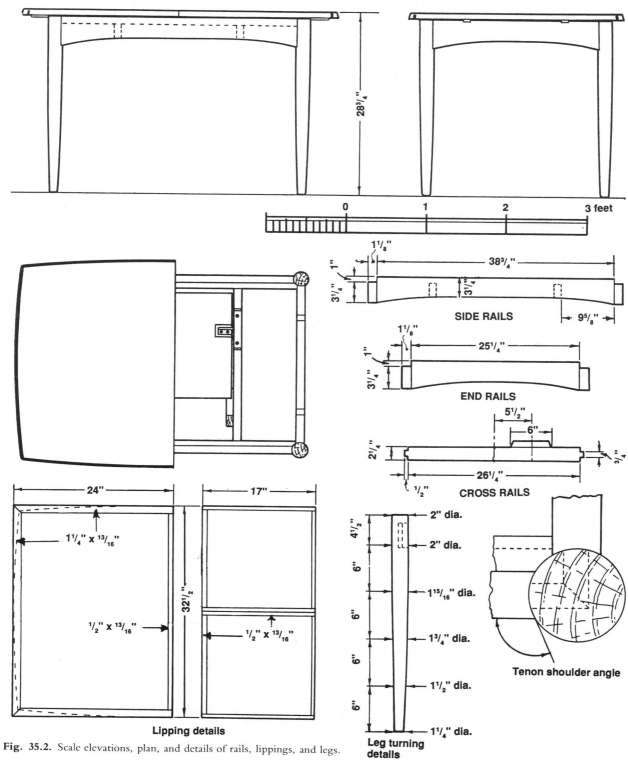

28³/₄"

0   1   2   3 feet

1¹/₈"
1"
3¹/₄"   38³/₄"   3¹/₄"   9⁵/₈"

SIDE RAILS

1¹/₈"
1"
3¹/₄"   25¹/₄"

END RAILS

5¹/₂"
6"
2¹/₄"   26¹/₄"   ³/₄"
¹/₂"

CROSS RAILS

24"

1¹/₄" x ¹³/₁₆"

¹/₂" x ¹³/₁₆"

32¹/₂"

17"

¹/₂" x ¹³/₁₆"

Lipping details

4¹/₂"   2" dia.
6"   2" dia.
6"   1¹⁵/₁₆" dia.
6"   1³/₄" dia.
6"   1¹/₂" dia.
6"   1¹/₄" dia.

Leg turning details

Tenon shoulder angle

Fig. 35.2. Scale elevations, plan, and details of rails, lippings, and legs.

considerable saving in time. Only the four outer corners of the lippings are mitred; when the glue has set the lippings may be planed down flush with the blockboard panel and the entire surface well glass-papered to a smooth finish.

VENEERING

When positioning the taped veneer leaves on the glued groundwork, be careful that the grain pattern will coincide when the large panels are placed together. It is advisable to use a backing veneer on the underside to compensate for any movement due to the 'pull' of the face veneer – any distortion of the top could result in the locating pegs and their sockets not engaging properly. When the glue has set the veneer can be glasspapered in the usual way.

Mark out and cut the curved edges of the two large panels, planing the edges to the bevel shown in Fig. 35.4. You will also need to trim the pair of centre panels to fit exactly between the two large panels, and the next step is to fit the pair of cylindrical hinges between the centre folding leaves.

SLIDERS

Groove the guides to receive the sliders as shown in Fig. 35.7; then glue and screw each one in position level with the top of the side rails. The shape of the sliders allows a small clearance between the frame and the underside of the top to minimise friction.

Note the four ¾in by ⁵⁄₁₆in strips which are screwed to the underside of the large panels and which slide in to support the weight of the top when it is closed they also ensure an easy opening action if the table is extended from the side. Glue a block of wood ½in long into the centre of the slot on each side to act as a stop for the sliders.

LOCATING PEGS

You can run into difficulties when fitting the pegs and sockets to the interlocking edges of the top panels, and you can avoid inaccuracies by making a simple drilling jig as shown in Fig. 35.5. This can be cramped to each of the four edges in turn and give you exact alignment.

Drill ¼in dia holes, ½in deep in every position;

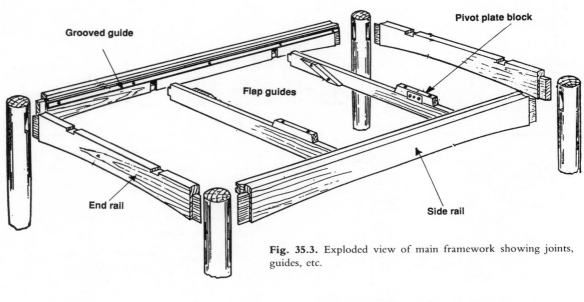

Fig. 35.3. Exploded view of main framework showing joints, guides, etc.

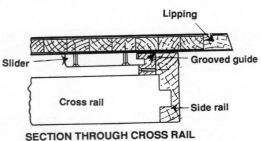

SECTION THROUGH CROSS RAIL

Fig. 35.4. How the tops slide.

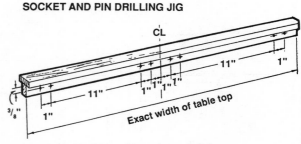

SOCKET AND PIN DRILLING JIG

Fig. 35.5. Jig for marking pins and sockets.

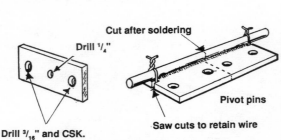

Fig. 35.6. Pivot pins and plates.

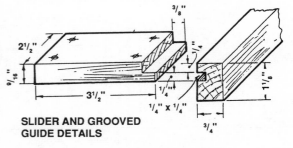

SLIDER AND GROOVED GUIDE DETAILS

Fig. 35.7. Sizes of sliders and guides.

those to receive sockets will have to be enlarged to
⅜in dia if they are to be bushed. You will also have
to drill the holes for the pins ¼in deeper, using a ⁷⁄₃₂in
drill.

You will need to make 16 sockets, ⁵⁄₁₆in long, cut
from ⅜in (outside dia) by ¼in (inside dia) brass tube.
If you find they are not a tight fit in the holes, use a
conical pointed nail punch to expand them while they
are in position.

Cut the ¼in dia brass pins 1⅛in long, and slightly
taper off about ¼in of the protruding end; this taper
can easily be filed while the pin is revolving in a lathe
or the chuck of an electric drill. When you tap the
pins into position they will be gripped tightly by the
smaller counterbored hole; if the ends of the sockets
protrude they can be countersunk with a rose counter-
sinking bit until they are flush.

FITTING THE TABLE TOP
Start by screwing the pivot plate blocks in position
on the cross rails before assembling the table top.
Then invert the table to fix the sliders with 1¼in by
10 c/s head screws; locate the centre sliders against
the groove stops and position the others to allow
each panel to move 9½in.

Because the pivot pins and plates are not standard
fittings, you will probably find it difficult to buy
them. However, it is a straightforward job to fabri-
cate them as shown in Fig. 35.6. The parts to be
joined should be cleaned, fluxed, and then wired
together, and heat can be applied until either the soft
or silver solder used melts to form a joint. Then saw
the fitting in half to make a pair.

With the table still inverted, fit the opened-out
extension leaf between the larger panels so that you
can screw the pivoting arrangement in position. The
pivot pins are mounted on pads ⅜in thick with the
centre of the pin 5½in from the hinged centre joint;
you can recess the pivot plates in which the pins
revolve flush into the blocks, if you wish, after you
have tested the action.

Note the pair of sloping guides screwed to the
centre rails to hold the folded flap level; they also lift

CUTTING LIST

	INCHES			MM		
	L	W	T	L	W	T
1 top	61	30	¾	1549	762	19
4 legs	29	2¼	2	739	58	51
2 side rails	41½	4½	1	1054	115	25
2 end rails	28	4½	1	711	115	25
2 cross rails	28	2½	1	711	64	25
2 grooved guides	40	1⅜	¾	1016	35	19
8 sliders	4	2½	⁹⁄₁₆	102	64	14
2 flap guides	7	1	¾	178	25	19
2 pivot blocks	6	1⅜	1	153	35	25
4 guide strips	12	1	⁵⁄₁₆	305	25	8
2 lippings	33	1½	¹³⁄₁₆	838	38	21
4 lippings	25	1½	¹³⁄₁₆	635	38	21
2 lippings	32	¾	¹³⁄₁₆	813	19	21
8 lippings	17½	¾	¹³⁄₁₆	445	19	21

Working allowances have been made to lengths and
widths; thicknesses are net.

the lower half over the side rail when the extension
is unfolded.

POLISHING
This is a recommended finish, involving the following processes. Mahogany wood filler was rubbed
well into the grain on the table frame with a piece of
coarse linen. After finally smoothing it off with flour
paper, three coats of amber French polish were
applied with a wide mop brush. Each coat, including
the last, was rubbed down with fine steel wool and
then its surface was lightly waxed.

The table top, however, was treated with two
coats of polyurethane lacquer. Both coats were
smoothed down with fine wet-and-dry paper, and
then finally brought to a dull sheen by cutting the
surface back with a burnishing cream.

PEMBROKE-STYLE DINING TABLE

Fig. 36.1. The table with the leaf down showing its shape – note the crossbanded edge.

The dimensions shown may be taken as a general guide but can be varied to suit individual requirements; thus, the length could vary from 36in to 42in. The structure consists basically of a box-like frame dovetailed together. Two legs are notched to fit at diagonally opposite corners and fixed with glue and screws (see Fig. 36.3, right). On the outside of each long side of the framework a fixed rail is screwed on, and a fly rail is pivoted to it by a knuckle joint. The moving leg is fixed to the fly rail with screws as in Figs. 36.3 and 36.5. To give a neat finish to the flaps and fixed top a rule joint is used with the rounded member veneered, thus giving a rich appearance; you may prefer to lip the top with satinwood and work the moulding in this without using veneer.

FRAMEWORK

Plain through-dovetail joints are used for the framework, which can be in any sound hardwood. The legs are planed to an octagonal section, tapered in length, and the hollow flutes worked with a spindle or a round moulding plane. Each pair of opposite flutes is veneered at the same time, round-faced cauls being used to apply pressure. Notches cut at the top of the legs enable them to fit to the framework and fly rails: note that the notches vary in size.

PIVOTED LEGS

Knuckle joints make the neatest and most reliable means of pivoting the fly rails, (B), Fig. 36.2, but you may prefer to make the metal pivots at (A). Or you could cut finger joints in wood – these have the advantage that they can be worked with saw and chisel: in both cases the metal pin is ³⁄₁₆in diameter. You will find it easiest to put the joint together, add the leg, finally screwing the fixed rail to the framework.

The bowed ends of the framework (Fig. 36.2) are not part of the construction but are made up and veneered separately, and fixed on with glue blocks at the back after polishing. The best way of making them is to laminate three pieces together, cramping them to a former; use the same former when veneering, bending and cramping the caul to it.

TOPS

These are of ¾in blockboard, veneered both sides, with a crossbanding and inlay line following the shape, and the edges are also veneered. As it is essential to present a clean, unbroken outline when the flaps are raised, you will need to work the rule joints first. You will have take care when working these, especially if the rounded edges are to be veneered. In the table shown, a 1⅛in dia dowel was veneered over about one third of its circumference; a hollow caul or a sandbag can be used to apply pressure. Once veneered, a precise flat must be planed on to the dowel to ¹⁄₁₆in below its centre, and the rebate shown in Fig. 36.6 can be worked.

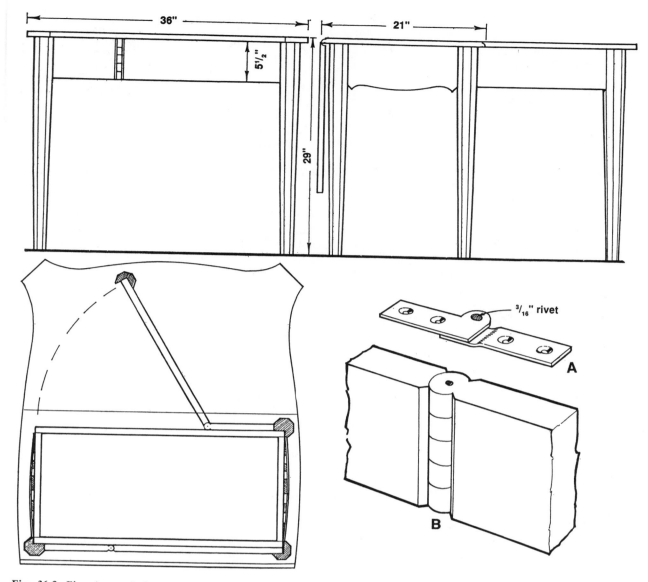

Fig. 36.2. Elevations and plan; also detail of (A) metal pivot, and (B) knuckle joint.

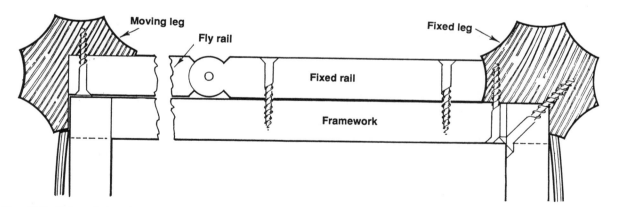

Fig. 36.3. Enlarged plan view to show how the legs fit to the frame.

You can spindle or use a scratchstock to work the hollows on the flaps, and all show edges should be veneered; use rule-joint hinges as ordinary back flaps are unsuitable.

VENEERING

Now mark out and cut the shapes, making sure that the edges are square. The flaps must be perfectly level before being veneered, so take a fine-set plane over the whole surface, followed by a toothing plane. If you are using a veneering hammer, both sides should be dealt with before the glue sets (especially in the case of Scotch glue); you will find it easier to employ cauls, however, the veneers being jointed and taped first. Both sides are pressed in a single operation. As there is a crossbanding it is advisable to allow the veneer to stand in slightly and add the banding later.

Once the glue has set, the edges can be trimmed

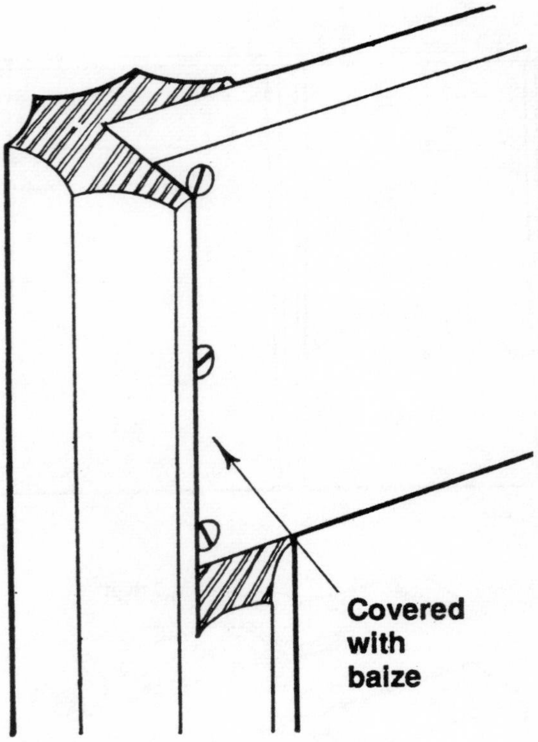
Covered
with
baize

Fig. 36.4. Showing joint of the leg to the fly rail.

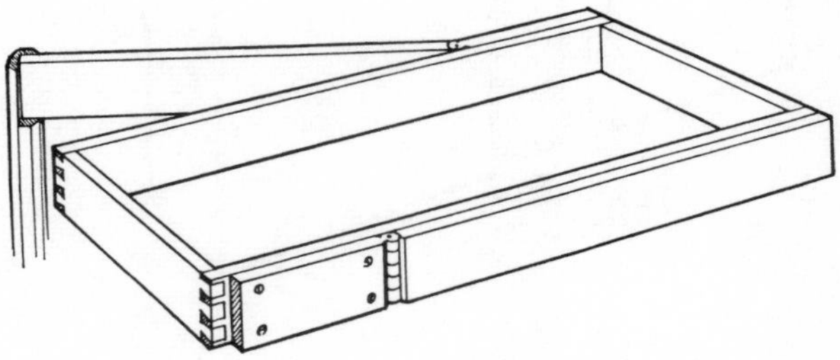

Fig. 36.5. How the box frame is made.

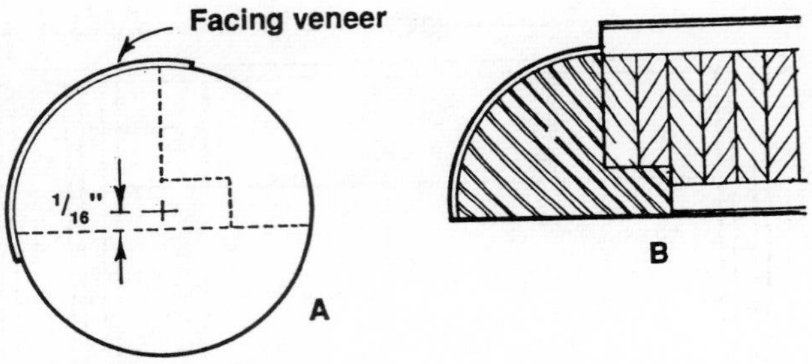
Facing veneer
1/16"
A
B

Fig. 36.6. How the rule joint is veneered and fitted.

and the crossbanding added, using a sharp cutting gauge to cut in the shape; you can then introduce the inner inlay line, and finally lay the crossbanding. After you have trimmed off any surplus, you can veneer the edges, and cut the rebate for the large outer inlay line with a cutting gauge. Incidentally, when veneering satinwood you will find it helpful to add a little flake white powder pigment to Scotch glue to lighten its colour.

CUTTING LIST

	INCHES			*MM*		
	L	W	T	L	W	T
1 top bed	36½	21¼	¾	927	540	19
2 flaps, each	36½	20¼	¾	927	515	19
4 legs, each	28⅝	3	2¾	728	76	70
2 long rails	32½	5¾	¾	825	146	19
2 short rails	15¾	6¼	¾	400	159	19
2 long fly rails	23	5¾	¾	584	146	19
2 short fly rails	9½	5¾	¾	241	146	19
2 bow ends, ply	16	6¼	3/16	407	159	5

Working allowances have been made to lengths and widths; thicknesses are net.

Acknowledgements

The Publisher would like to thank the following for the inclusion of their designs in this book.

1 Medieval Aumbry *P Barton*
2 Gelderland Drop-Leaf Table *Rene Coolen*
3 Jacobean-Style Draw Table *Author unknown*
4 Dining Table with Shaped Standard Ends *J. Shackleton*
5 Trestle Table with Standard Ends *Author unknown*
6 Oak Tripod Table with a Tilting Top *Rene Coolen*
7 Dining Table with Shaped End Frames *F. Haynes*
8 Hepplewhite-Style Serving Cabinet *R. Irving*
9 Wall Cupboard *J. Robinson*
10 Double Cake Stand *Author unknown*
11 Cupboard Dresser *S. Hurrell*
12 Lancashire-Style Dresser *G. Rendel*
13 Pitch Pine Dresser *M. Evans*
14 Dresser with Glazed Cupboards *T. Lord*
15 Modern Dresser with Swivelling TV Table *Author unknown*
16 A Pack-Flat Table *Author unknown*
17 Snack Stand *N. Place*
18 Food Preparation Wagon *A. Hontoir*
19 Sutherland Gateleg Table *A. Pearce*
20 Gateleg Dining Table without Underframing *A. Pearce*
21 Teak Sideboard with Part-Tambour Front *A. Rodgers*
22 A 'Running Sideboard' or Dinner Wagon *Author unknown*
23 Tea Trolley *T. Waite*
24 Loose-Leaf Extending Table *Author unknown*
25 Sideboard in Teak *K. Farrington*
26 Extending Dining Table with Loose Leaf *Author unknown*
27 Sculptured Tea Wagon *G. Arstall*
28 Dining Table with Automatic Rising Central Leaf *Author unknown*
29 Sideboard with Tambour-Fronted Cupboards *A. Watson*
30 Easy-to-Make Dinner Wagon *G. Warr*
31 Sideboard with Mirror-Lined Cocktail Cabinet *R. Morton*
32 An Elegant Sideboard with Maximum Storage *S. Sandham*
33 Circular Dining Table *O. Wood*
34 Two Tables from One Basic Design *C. Colston*
35 Extending Dining Table *K. Wells*
36 Pembroke-Style Dining Table *H. Donkin*

MAKING OUR MARK IN

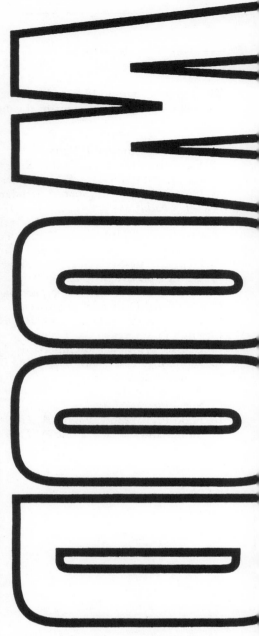

August 1990 £1.50

Woodworker
Britain's best-selling woodwork magazine

DAVID FIELD
Design for production

LUCINDA LEECH
Design for conservation

Sheffield steeled

Ornamental woodwork

ISSN 0043-776X

If you're interested in crafts and craftsmanship why not try Britain's top selling magazine for woodwork enthusiasts?

WOODWORKER is bright-looking, lively, with lots of colour and carries approximately one hundred pages each issue. Inside you'll find a wide range of projects to make, from the simple to the really challenging in cabinetmaking, woodturning and carving. There's also more articles on general topics of wood-related interest than any other magazine in the field.

WOODWORKER has its roots in the past – it started in 1901 – but it's bang up to date on new materials, new techniques and new designs, as well as drawing inspiration from the past.

You'll find a fascinating selection of readers' letters, expert answers to common problems and readers' own ingenious ideas.

Most importantly, the magazine is staffed by people who know and love wood. When woodwork is our pride and our passion it's bound to be reflected in the pages we produce. Perhaps that's the reason why WOODWORKER is Britain's number one.

Take out a subscription to WOODWORKER and join thousands of other satisfied subscribers who enjoy the privilege of having their favourite specialist magazine delivered to their homes POST FREE*!